When Your Child Starts School

A handbook for concerned parents

SU GARNETT

How To Books

Published by How To Books Ltd,
3 Newtec Place, Magdalen Road,
Oxford, OX4 1RE, United Kingdom.
Tel: (01865) 793806. Fax: (01865) 248780.
info@howtobooks.co.uk
www.howtobooks.co.uk

First edition 2001

British Library Cataloguing in Publication Data
A catalogue record for this book is available from
the British Library.

Edited by Julie Nelson
Cartoons by Mike Flanagan
Cover design by Shireen Nathoo Design
Cover image PhotoDisc

Produced for How To Books by Deer Park Productions
Typeset by Anneset, Weston-super-Mare, North Somerset
Printed and bound by Cromwell Press, Trowbridge, Wiltshire

Note: The material contained in this book is set out in good
faith for general guidance and no liability can be accepted
for loss or expense incurred as a result of relying in particular
circumstances on statements made in the book. The laws and
regulations are complex and liable to change, and readers should
check the current position with the relevant authorities before
making personal arrangements.

Contents

Preface   9

1 Choosing Schools   **13**

    What to consider   13
    Your first visit   14
    Asking the right questions   16
    Making your choice   18
    Summary   19

2 Settling In to the New School   **20**

    Surviving the first morning   20
    The parent/teacher relationship   21
    Understanding the first day   24
    Understanding the first week   25
    Understanding the curriculum   26
    Summary   27

3 Recognising Children's Problems   **29**

    Early difficulties   29
    Common complaints from children   31
    Difficult feelings for children   32
    Case study   35
    Other common complaints about school   36
    Parents' complaints and difficulties   37
    Summary   38

4 Responsibilities of Parents and Teachers   **39**

    What does the teacher expect from you?   39
    What does the teacher expect the children to be able to do?   42
    Understanding Baseline Assessment   44

What should you expect from your child's teacher? 44

5 Adapting to School **48**

Understanding the parent's role 48
Helping children to develop the right attitude to learning 49
Case study 55
Helping children to make friends 55
Case study 57
Helping children to get on with their teacher 59

6 Retaining Home Links **64**

What do children need their new teacher to do? 64
Creating a successful working environment 65
Making school exciting and fun 69
Building self-esteem 76

7 Maintaining Good Relationships **82**

Giving mutual support and admiration 82
Having truly positive exchanges 82
Recognising emotions 83
Acknowledging a fear of criticism 83
Tackling problems early 83
Questions and answers 84

8 Vital Developments for the Future **88**

Developing a sense of humour and an ability to laugh 88
Developing confidence 89
Case study 90
Developing tolerance 92
Developing reliability 92
Developing patience 93
Developing empathy 94

9 Personal Reflections 95

Being a teacher of young children 95
Being a parent of young children 95

Appendix 1 – Advice on packed lunches 97
Appendix 2 – Literacy and Numeracy Hours 99

Appendix 3 – Sample Report   101
Appendix 4 – Home/School Contracts   103

Glossary   105

Further Reading   109

Useful Addresses and Web sites   113

Index   117

Preface

PROMOTING UNDERSTANDING BETWEEN HOME AND SCHOOL

This book is written for both parents and teachers of young children. It is also written for teacher trainers and teacher trainees.

As a parent, I fully understand the many difficulties and frustrations of bringing up a young family. I am also only too aware of the mistakes I have made over the years. (I am glad to say that my children have no qualms about telling me!) More recently, as a teacher of Early Years children, I have experienced the difficulties and frustrations from the 'other side' as it were. This has led me to believe strongly that home and school are inextricably linked and that partnerships between parents and teachers are both crucial and invaluable.

Although relations between parents and teachers are becoming, on the whole, less formal and more comfortable, there is still a certain amount of unease between them. As it is vital for both parties to understand where each is coming from, I have designed this book to reflect both parents' and teachers' viewpoints. It is important to consider both of these.

For parents, the end of the pre-school era can be a time of great sadness. They have grown used to having their child around and can find it very difficult when they go off to school for the first time. This is not only a stressful time, but can also be a time when many are prone to feelings of guilt, especially if their children are not used to being left for long periods of time and therefore take a while to settle. That stress is often aggravated by a lack of knowledge about what actually happens in school. This book is designed to minimise these negative feelings by dispelling myths and providing information in a simple, jargon-free, parent-friendly form.

SHARING INFORMATION AND BUILDING TRUST

The start of the school year can be equally stressful and difficult for teachers as they try to settle everyone in, remember new names and establish a successful, working routine. Their job can be made much easier with the help of relevant information provided by you.

When children begin school, they quickly come to depend on their teacher as well as their parents. School becomes another significant place in their lives. It is natural for both parents and teachers, home and school, to be equally important to them. Therefore, it is extremely helpful if parents and teachers can work together as partners, each with vital roles in setting up home/school links. Throughout the book, I have pinpointed the links between home and school.

It is very important that your child sees his school as a happy place. Teachers are allies and friends and should be seen as such. This book will provide you with suggestions for establishing good, friendly relationships with your child's teacher. This is very helpful for your child and it will also help you to build your relationship with the teacher into one of mutual trust and respect. This will make the vital business of finding out about and becoming involved in your child's education much easier.

Parents know their children better than anyone else and can provide teachers with vital and useful information. With the development of a good relationship of trust between parents and teachers, this valuable source can be used productively.

DEVELOPING PERSONAL AND SOCIAL SKILLS

As interested parents, it is fully recognised that you will already be doing everything you can to make your children feel valued and important. These essential feelings of self-esteem will help your children to work and play successfully with their peers when they start school. It is obviously beneficial if the experiences young children have at home are helpful to them when they begin school and this book explains how to develop this approach.

Invaluable social skills such as sharing, becoming independent, showing consideration for others and so on need to be nurtured during the 'Early Years'. Children learn a tremendous amount through informal 'play' and by example and this needs to be developed in the school setting.

Children will become good children themselves if they see their parents, teachers and peers as positive role models. If parents and teachers help children to develop a healthy self-esteem and encourage early development of these important social skills, the children in their care are more likely to grow up to be young adults who are confident and have positive and tolerant attitudes towards others. It is, of course, recognised that some children do not respond easily or immediately in this way, despite our very best endeavours. They are difficult, they remain difficult and it is then very hard to keep reacting positively. However, I am a firm believer in the fact that if you keep trying to implement the right kind of strategies, even though it can often feel as if you are banging your head against a brick wall, some of the love, care and attention will eventually sink in and reap rewards. It is the early development of these social skills that this book is trying to address.

GAINING CONFIDENCE

By the time you reach the end of this book, you should hopefully be feeling a high degree of confidence about your ability to provide children with the necessary tools to make their early days at school, and their subsequent progression through it, a happy and positive experience for all of you – child, parents and teacher alike. You should also be feeling well equipped to deal with any difficulties that will inevitably arise from time to time.

When that important (or dreaded!) first day dawns, you will be able to take a deep breath, put your best foot forward with confidence and set off with enthusiasm. Your child should pick up your air of confidence (be it real, or perhaps a little enforced at this stage!) and feel secure in the certainty that all will be well and that this is a totally natural step for him to be taking. The transition from home to school will have happened with relative ease.

A NOTE ON LANGUAGE

The focus of the book is the parent/teacher relationship. Throughout the text, for ease of use, I have referred to your child as 'he' and the teacher as 'she'. All thoughts and suggestions are equally valid for both sexes. In addition, any reference to parents clearly refers to both mothers and fathers and may well be of interest and use to grandparents and others who care for these young children.

ACKNOWLEDGEMENTS

Thank you to my husband, Christopher, for his constant support and patience during the development of this book, and to my three children, Lucy, Emma and Simon for giving me so much happiness – and guidance – over the years. Special thanks must also go to many friends, relatives and colleagues who have inspired me and given me such invaluable help.

Su Garnett

1

Choosing Schools

WHAT TO CONSIDER

Many children, from the age of 2+, attend pre-schools, nurseries or play-groups which may or may not be linked to their main school. Choosing a school for your child, be it at 2+ or at 4+ or, indeed, at any age, is an extremely important task. Many aspects need to be considered and careful judgements made but I believe there are two basic rules:

1. Make sure you ask everything you want to in order to be able to make an informed choice.

2. Trust your own gut feelings and judgement. It can be useful to hear what other parents have to say about their experiences of the school, but ultimately it is your own impressions that really matter.

Before you start looking at possibilities, consider what you want your child to gain from his education. List everything, for example:

- confidence
- independence
- academic/sporting/creative success
- friendships
- enthusiasm
- self-esteem
- tolerance
- empathy
- good manners.

Then consider carefully your own child:

- Does he need gentle encouragement or does he respond well to pressure?
- Is he gregarious or shy?
- What are his interests?
- Does he have any special needs or health problems?

Do the schools you are considering sound as if they would meet your requirements (as defined above)? Look carefully at their location with regard to journey time from home and work. When you have narrowed down your choice and are interested in a school, ring or write to arrange a visit.

YOUR FIRST VISIT

When you visit the school, your first impressions are all important. These will probably be very similar to those of your child so feel justified in trusting your judgement when you finally make the choice for him. One of the most important things is to be greeted by smiling, welcoming faces. If this is one of the first impressions of the school, it will immediately help to put you at ease. The atmosphere is equally important and will give you a very good indication of the aims of the school, the quality of teaching and the behaviour and attitude of the pupils. If you are also greeted by light, bright, colourful rooms rather than gloomy, unexciting ones, this will undoubtedly add to your positive feelings.

Looking around the waiting area

Obviously, not every school has the benefit of a purpose-built building or, indeed, plenty of money to spend on decoration, but there are other ways to make a school look bright and cheerful. If you have to wait to meet the Head, have a look around the waiting area:

- Bearing in mind that the first priority may be for money to be spent on books and equipment, does the building look clean and looked after?
- Are there any displays or pictures on the walls?
- Are there any ornaments, flowers or items the children have made on the table or shelves?

- Are there any comfortable chairs where you are waiting?

- Do you have anything to look at – Prospectus, children's written work or photographs of school events?

If the answer to any of these questions is no, ask yourself why.

What to look for as you go round

- Watch how children react to the Head. Do they talk to her in an excited way or do they fall silent?

- Are you introduced to your child's future teacher and are you allowed to talk to her? (This will obviously depend somewhat on what is happening in her class at the time.)

- Look at the displays. What are they like? Be suspicious if they look too perfect and ask yourself who has done them. Can you identify children's work (paintings, drawings or writing) in them? If not, again ask yourself why. If all writing on the displays has been word-processed on the computer, has it been done by the children? Tell-tale signs to show that it hasn't include no spelling mistakes, no incorrect spacing and no lower-case letters where there should be capitals! You and all the children in the class should be able to see their own work displayed, corrected as necessary by the teacher but not rewritten by her. If only perfect work is displayed, this sends a very negative message to the less able child. Look for examples of everyone's work on the walls, not just the best.

- Is the classroom well organised, i.e. is it conducive to productive work? This is not the same as having a tidy classroom. Some untidiness is inevitable in a productive classroom. Is there enough space to move around easily? Do the children have plenty of room in which to work and play and are the chairs and tables at a comfortable height for them?

- Are the children happily occupied? Are they willing to talk to you and explain what they are doing? There should ideally be a contented hum in the room – not silence and not too much noise (depending on the lesson, obviously).

- Are there plenty of interesting things – they don't have to be expensive - within easy reach of the children, for them to handle and examine?

- Are there plenty of well-looked after books?
- Is there an ABC chart and a number chart displayed on the walls?
- Is there a parents' noticeboard?
- Were you made to feel welcome and were you met with a smile by everyone you saw?

You should now have a good idea as to whether this is the school for you and your child. If you are feeling it might well be, now is the time to ask all those questions to help you clarify any concerns.

ASKING THE RIGHT QUESTIONS

Having looked carefully around the school, you will have gained a very good idea about what goes on inside. Carefully chosen, open-ended questions will help you to find out more and assess whether the school can give your child the kind of support and encouragement he needs. The type of information you want will obviously depend on your personal circumstances but you might like to consider the following areas:

1. *Aims*. What are the aims of the school? Are you given a clear answer? (Although written aims and objectives may well contain jargon, you should rightly expect that jargon to be translated when receiving a verbal answer!)

2. *Expectations*. What do you expect children to be able to do when they arrive at your school?

3. *Maintaining interest*. How do you ensure that children remain stimulated by and interested in their school work?

4. *Flexibility*. How much flexibility can be built into your Early Years Curriculum?

5. *Different abilities*. How do you cater for different abilities and interests when teaching the children?

6. *Individuality*. How do teaching methods at the school build up the strengths of each individual child?

7. *Extension and support*. How do you extend your more able pupils while providing the necessary support for others in the class?

8. *The wider curriculum*. What areas do you consider to be of vital

importance outside the formal academic curriculum? (For example sharing, consideration for others, politeness, etc.)

9. *Encouraging independence.* How do you help the children to become independent in both work and play?

10. *Reluctant learners.* How do you encourage the reluctant learner or the child who finds things hard?

11. *Special help.* Do you have additional, specialised, individual help for children who are falling behind or need plenty of reinforcement?

12. *The uninterested child.* What strategies do you have for helping the uninterested child or the child who finds it hard to settle?

13. *Allergies.* How is the school set up to deal with children's health allergies, such as hayfever, eczema, asthma, nut and other food allergies?

14. *Disabilities.* Are there any facilities for disabled children?

15. *Care facilities.* Are there any before – and after – school care facilities?

16. *School meals.* Do the children have a cooked meal at lunchtime? Can you see a sample menu?

17. *Rules.* What rules are imposed? (Are these too controlling?)

18. *Discipline.* What kind of discipline do you use?

If you are considering keeping your child at this school for quite a few years to come, think about his needs in the years ahead as well as his needs now. For example:

- If he is sporty, do they have adequate sporting facilities?
- If he is musical, can he learn an instrument at an early stage?

Listen carefully to replies and ask follow-up questions if you are not satisfied with the first answer.

Thinking about the school's response to you
- Are you given plenty of time to ask your questions or are you left feeling hassled and hurried?
- Are you looked at directly and shaken firmly by the hand as you leave?

MAKING YOUR CHOICE

You now have plenty to consider and will need time to mull everything over. However, you can rest assured that after this time of careful consideration, you will have made your choice based on careful assessment and should be feeling confident and happy about this next important step for your child.

Over-Subscribed Schools

Although you are encouraged and advised to express a choice about which school you wish your child to attend, if you choose a school which is heavily over-subscribed, there is no guarantee that you will be offered a place. Most over-subscribed schools use a number of criteria for allocating places. These vary but may well be based on such issues as:

1. Whether there are siblings already at the school
2. Proximity to the school.
3. Whether the family is actively involved in the church community, if it is a church school.

It is a good idea to check the latest information with individual schools. Some Independent schools select at this age, while others do not.

Moving to another school

Obviously, no one can guarantee that you have chosen the right school for your child and no one can guarantee that everything will work out as you wish it to. If things go wrong, it is always possible for you to make the move to another school, but it is probably unwise to do this hastily, without trying to sort out any problems which may have arisen at the current school. However, if you are convinced that there is a fundamental problem which cannot be addressed, try to move your child at the end of a school year. There are obviously times when making a move in the middle of the year cannot be avoided – for example when families relocate – but this can be very disruptive for child, class and teacher.

Pre-visits

Having registered your child in the school of your choice, you and he should ideally be invited to spend some time with the teacher in his new classroom before he formally starts school.

SUMMARY

- Consider your needs carefully beforehand.
- Make sure you observe and listen very carefully when you visit.
- Don't be afraid to ask.
- 'Listen' to your gut reactions and feelings.
- Feel confident about your decision.

2

Settling In to the New School

SURVIVING THE FIRST MORNING

Having carefully chosen your child's school and arranged one or more pre-visits with your child, you should be feeling happy about your choice. Relax in the knowledge that the Reception class teachers will have put much thought into making the new school atmosphere welcoming.

What to expect

You will undoubtedly notice some or all of the following:

● clear notices to direct you to classrooms and cloakrooms

● coat pegs and tables or desks clearly marked with children's names

● bright, welcoming posters on the walls

● a variety of interesting things for your children to look at and handle

● plenty of familiar and new toys for children to play with

● smiling teachers, ready to get down (literally!) to the children's level in order to talk to them.

Children will immediately be made to feel welcome. Teachers will be every bit as determined as you to make your child feel happy and confident in his new environment.

What can you do to help?

Trust teachers and let them get on with the settling-in process. Say goodbye to your child warmly but firmly, stating that you will be back to collect him at the end of the day and leave quickly. If your child protests, please try not to linger. Many years of experience have reinforced my opinion that children almost always respond positively and quickly to diversionary tactics as soon as alternatives (in the form of parents) are removed.

THE PARENT/TEACHER RELATIONSHIP

It is important to consider this relationship on your child's first morning. Both parents and teachers are working towards the same goal. How much easier it will be to reach this goal if they can build up a relationship of trust and talk to each other easily. With luck, all will go smoothly on your child's first morning and you will be able to leave him quickly and easily and feel totally happy about doing so. If this is the case, your relationship with the teacher will already be on a good footing.

When things go wrong

It may, however, be that you arrive with your child, determined to make this a positive experience for both of you and determined not to let any of your own fears show. He is feeling nervous, you are hoping that your 'steel' will last. You arrive at the same time as several other parents, the teacher is busy talking to one of them, you are not sure what to do. Your child starts clinging to you. How are you feeling? Stressed, let-down, angry, worried. Not a good start to a trusting and easy relationship with your child's teacher!

The teacher has a new class of x children, all probably somewhat nervous and at least some likely to be upset when their parents leave. She has the same or possibly double the number of new parents, some of whom are also likely to find the separation difficult. She is very anxious to be welcoming and to make everyone feel special and at home. Perhaps she has no other assistance and everyone is arriving within a very short space of time. How is she feeling? Stressed, anxious, rude, uncaring, pulled in umpteen different directions at once. Not a good start either!

It is clear that the time to build the initial relationship with your child's teacher is not now, on the first morning, but during visits to the school before your child actually starts. Those earlier occasions allow you time to ask any questions you want to and give your child a chance to acquaint himself with his new surroundings and to get to know his teacher.

Clarifying your role – preparation

- *Be well prepared!* You should have been told, in writing, exactly what your child will need for school. Make sure you act on this.

- *Read letters carefully,* absorb the information and clarify any queries straight away.

- *Provide emergency contact numbers.* Give these to your child's teacher. It will help you to feel confident about leaving him if you plan your movements on his first day so that you can be contacted easily should this prove necessary.

- *Find out where the loos and cloakrooms are* when you visit the school initially so that you can show your child if necessary.

- *Talk to your child about what to expect* when you take him to his new school for his first day. At your particular school, it may be that there is a set procedure for children to follow as they arrive. If this is the case, make sure you go through this with your child. Otherwise, tell him exactly what *you* will do and stick to it. This will help your child to feel secure and will also help you to avoid those guilty feelings following, as both you and your child see it, uncharacteristic or unexpected behaviour. If the teacher is busy with other children and parents, you will:

  - help him to hang up his things on his peg
  - find his place in the classroom
  - help him to settle himself down and get involved in the activity that has been put out for him.

You will then leave and pick him up again later in the day. (Make sure you are not late – otherwise you will undo all your good work!)

Make it clear that, if the teacher is free, she is likely to be around as well, helping, while he settles in.

Your role on the first morning

- *Make sure you bring everything* that you have been asked to bring.

- *Be on time!* If you arrive after most of the other children in the class, you are putting your child at a disadvantage. He may well feel very conspicuous and embarrassed if he is the last person to arrive and has to walk in when the register is being taken or when all the other children are ready and waiting. Many adults still find it very daunting to walk into a room full of people, so why should a child feel any differently? When you are trying to give the message that school is an exciting and happy place to be, to put him in this position is not fair and will not help you to settle him. In my experience, children who arrive late always find it harder to get used to school than those who are given plenty of time to get organised and to say goodbye calmly.

● *Be prepared to hang up coats* and find pegs and places with your child. If your teacher is free when you arrive, or she has an assistant, one of them will obviously help with all this. If she is busy, it will help her enormously if you can deal with the 'mechanics' of arriving yourself, sit your child down and involve him in whatever has been put out for him (drawing, puzzles, etc.). Hopefully, he will then become relatively comfortable with the whole process and settle more easily than you thought, in which case you can help the teacher by occupying as little of her time as possible and withdrawing quickly on this particular morning. This will release her to be able to comfort and reassure those children who are less confident, including yours, if this becomes necessary.

Understanding the teacher's role

In order to manage this first morning successfully the teacher needs to:

● be well prepared

● make the classroom as welcoming as possible with interesting things for the children to do

● welcome and include all parents, trying to talk to them all, being brief but not brusque

● share herself amongst all the children, acknowledging and smiling at them all, but paying particular attention to the most vulnerable at this time.

Enjoying a successful outcome

Having thought about and seen the situation from each other's point of view, both parents and teachers should now be feeling much happier about their relationship.

● They are beginning to recognise constraints on both sides and are already building up both trust and understanding.

● They are exercising give and take and automatically helping one another.

As a parent, how are you feeling now?

If you have a confident child and have been able to leave him happily, you will probably be feeling more comfortable. You have understood the pressures the teacher is under, you have been able to help by freeing her to attend to other children and this has hopefully left you feeling good. If you have a worried child, you should be feeling looked after and helped. The teacher has recognised your child's need for particular attention and plenty of reassurance at this time and this has left you feeling less tense and understood. Tomorrow, it may well be the other way round.

The teacher should be feeling more in control and able to do her job. You now have a sound basis for building up a good relationship.

UNDERSTANDING THE FIRST DAY

Generally, the first day at school will be pretty informal. The register will be taken once all the children have settled. Children will probably have this procedure explained to them and will then be encouraged (not forced!) to answer for themselves. The children will have plenty of time to explore the classroom and its contents and will probably be taken on a tour to see where the loos, cloakroom, hall, dining room and play-ground are. They will be taken through the general routine of a normal day, including what happens at lunchtime and, if appropriate, shown other parts of the school. The teacher will probably try to spend some time in one-to-one discussion with each child in order to get to know them a little better. If you have provided the teacher with information about your child, she will certainly be bearing this in mind when talking to him. On the whole, teachers will concentrate on making the day as friendly and easy as possible. Do make sure that your child is not expecting to learn to read on his first day. This process tends to take a little longer!

Meeting your child after his first day at school

When you collect your child at the end of his first day, be sensitive to the fact that he will probably be very tired. Allow him time to relax before asking him anything. Instead, talk to him yourself, pointing out things in the classroom and suggesting what he might be doing tomorrow.

Talking a little about 'tomorrow' is quite a good idea as it is not unknown for children to think they have 'done' school once they have been there for only one day!

Relaxed conversation like this will probably be a relief to him and a welcome distraction for you when you are longing to ask him all sorts of questions. If you ask your child what he did at school today as soon as you see him, he will invariably tell you 'nothing'! Rest assured, this is always very far from the truth. It is much more likely that his day has been so packed, he is unable to single out any particular event to tell you about until he has had time to unwind. Even then, it may still seem to him a rather jumbled experience at this stage. This will make it very difficult for him to describe anything to anyone, however close.

Try not to feel excluded. This book is written in order to keep you informed about what is going on at school, even when your child won't tell you. It is obviously very important to distinguish between your child's reluctance to provide you with detailed information about his day and his reluctance to tell you about something which is clearly troubling him. The latter needs to be pursued, whereas it is probably wiser to ignore the former, at least initially.

UNDERSTANDING THE FIRST WEEK

Having survived his first day, your child will hopefully be feeling reassured and, if not exactly settled, at least less wary of his new environment. Some children never look back from this point onwards. However, others find the next few days just as, or even more, challenging, especially if they have not realised that school days are here to stay! For all, the rest of their first week will continue to provide them with plenty of new experiences and they need to have these carefully explained to them.

Understanding new experiences

It is important that the teacher does not assume that children will automatically understand when she asks them to do something. We know exactly what is meant by PE and Singing but children may well not and even if they do, they will not know what this means they have to do. New experiences may include any of the following:

- changing clothes/shoes and going from the classroom to the hall for PE

- going to the hall for Singing or Dance

- changing clothes/shoes and walking/going in a coach to the games field

- going to other rooms to watch television or use computers

- visiting the library

- being taught or supervised by other teachers

- eating with lots of noise, other children and strange food.

Children need to know exactly what is expected of them on each of these occasions to dispel their anxieties and uncertainties and to make them feel comfortable. They need time to learn the school routine. It is not necessary to make a big deal out of these new experiences which will soon become very familiar, but it is important that children know what to do and that the teacher checks their understanding by asking them. After the first full week, the routine will not change significantly and, therefore, it will not be necessary to keep explaining what to do, as long as the initial explanations have been well done.

UNDERSTANDING THE CURRICULUM

Children from the age of three in pre-school settings, be they playgroups or nurseries, will have largely followed a curriculum that is endeavouring to deliver the **Early Learning Goals**. Currently, there are six goals, namely:

- Personal, Social and Emotional Development

- Communication, Language and Literacy

- Mathematical Development

- Knowledge and Understanding of the World

- Physical Development

- Creative Development.

Children will continue to follow this **Foundation Stage** when they start in the Reception class of their main school, although it may be delivered in a progressively more formal way. After this first year, from the age of six, they will start to follow a curriculum based largely on the **National Curriculum**. There are ten subjects in the National Curriculum, namely:

- English

- Mathematics

- Science
- Design and Technology
- Information Technology
- History
- Geography
- Art
- Music
- Physical Education.

What will the change of curriculum mean for your child? The basic difference is not in the breadth of their learning, but in the depth of it and in the degree of formality with which it is delivered. Children at their main school will spend lots more time each day learning how to read and write (English) and how to use numbers (Mathematics) (See Appendix 2, Literacy and Numeracy Hours). They will also continue to learn all about the world around them – both now and in the past (Geography, History and Science). They will learn how to use computers (Information Technology) and will be taught how to design and make things in DT (Design and Technology). They will keep fit by taking part in games and PE (Physical Education) and they will learn to appreciate Art and Music in their creative sessions. Religious Education will also form part of the curriculum and they may well begin to learn a foreign language. Learning how to interact successfully with others both at work and at play (Personal, Social and Emotional Development) is still a vital part of the curriculum and will now include learning how to co-operate with others in group work.

Many parts of the Foundation Stage curriculum are delivered within the framework of a **topic** which allows teachers to build on children's experiences. Topics are specifically chosen so that the children will be able to join in and make contributions, bring objects from home and involve other members of their families. If children have a good basic understanding of a subject, they are in a much better position to be able to learn new information.

SUMMARY

- Be well prepared.
- Be on time.

- Make sure your child is well briefed.
- Trust the teacher.
- Recognise the two-way nature of a successful parent/teacher relationship.
- Be involved in your child's learning.

3

Recognising Children's Problems

EARLY DIFFICULTIES

Most young children take time to settle fully into their new school environment and almost all are bound to experience some frustrations and difficulties along the way. This book is designed to help build up good relationships between parents, teachers and children and to tackle everyday difficulties which may get in the way of those good relationships. It is not, however, attempting to offer advice on specific problems, such as dyslexia, dyspraxia, attention deficit disorder or severe cases of bullying. These are areas where there is plenty of specialist, expert help available. If you suspect that your child needs extra support because of any of these problems, seek advice as soon as possible, initially through the school. If necessary, this can be taken further by contacting organisations such as The Dyslexia Institute and The Dyspraxia Foundation or by consulting some of the excellent books which have been written by experts with a wealth of experience in these fields. (See the sections on further reading, useful addresses and websites at the end of the book).

Facing every day problems

The type of difficulties I am looking at here are common, everyday ones:

- peers teasing
- possessions being taken and not returned
- peers not sharing
- peers not including others in their games.

These problems arise for most children and because they occur frequently, it is helpful for children to be able to deal with them by themselves. Undoubtedly for some children, these difficulties can sometimes be very traumatic and can threaten their confidence and self-esteem.

However, as parents, teachers and capable adults, we should be trying to help children to develop ways of dealing with situations that they find difficult. We need to constantly build children's confidence and self-esteem so that if they do take a knock following an incident of the type described above, they have a reserve on which to draw. This should help them keep their problems more in perspective.

Helping children to cope with their problems

It is appropriate to acknowledge and discuss a problem your child has had, but it is also important to react in a sensible, balanced way to incidents of this sort – not over-reacting, but not dismissing them either. Children need to realise that they are responsible for their own actions and that these may also have contributed to the problem. When discussing what has happened, help your child to look at his part in the incident:

● Was he truly the innocent party?

● What was the build-up to what happened?

● Is there a reason why the other child might have acted as he did?

Encouraging this kind of discussion is not to suggest that your child is always in the wrong. It may well be that he has been treated unkindly and that the other child has been very unfair. However, it is probably wise not to assume that your child is always in the right.

Developing coping strategies

Helping children to think about what has happened is important and teaches them that there are many ways of dealing with frustrations and annoyances, some which aggravate the situation and others which improve it. Hopefully, children will gradually learn to cope with their problems by using strategies which result in fewer conflicts. This will further boost their confidence and self-esteem.

While problems remain relatively minor and common, they are often best dealt with in this fairly matter-of-fact, yet supportive way, even if you feel strongly that your child has been a victim of someone else's thoughtlessness. Our aim, as parents and teachers, is surely to help children to integrate happily with others in their social group and to help them to deal with things which upset them. The earlier they can find a way of coping for themselves, the easier it will be for them long term.

Responding to more serious problems

If there is a persistent, serious problem involving your child, this is obviously a very different matter. When occasional teasing turns into bullying, this needs much more detailed discussion with everyone concerned, careful thought and expert help. I am not attempting to offer that here, other than to advise you to go, without delay, straight to your child's teacher in such circumstances, so that these procedures can immediately be put into action.

COMMON COMPLAINTS FROM CHILDREN

'A took my toy without asking me and she won't give it back.'
'B's being horrid to me. She said I looked silly with my plaits.'
'C wouldn't let me play with her at playtime – she was playing with D and E.'

Of course, there will be times when your child will feel very upset by something that has happened at school and it is obviously right to comfort him and talk it through. Children must be allowed to complain and they should be encouraged to say what is wrong. It is important to listen to their problems and to make them feel that you understand, but it is then equally important to encourage them to 'move on'. Try to keep a sense of proportion about the whole issue and relay this to your child. Beware of taking sides against another pupil, because you are not really doing your child any favours by reacting in such a way.

Dealing with those complaints

Dwelling on an unfairness, as children see it, is not generally very helpful, but empathising with children and helping them to tackle diffi-culties constructively (as suggested above) increases the likelihood of their being able to cope with these frustrations by themselves in the future. As a general rule, it is a mistake to try to fight children's battles for them. If necessary, it is certainly better for your child to involve his teacher than to ask you to get involved.

- When his toy is taken without his permission, your child might try asking for it back calmly, before involving his teacher. If necessary, she could perhaps suggest to the child who has taken the toy, that he might not like it if someone took something belonging to him without asking. It has to be said that unless specifically requested by the teacher, for a particular project or event, it is much better if precious toys are not brought into school at all. It invariably causes problems and, very often, the toys get lost or damaged in some way. Although it is obviously good for children to learn how to share, this is better done with school equipment in school. If anything is brought into school for a specific occasion, it should be clearly named. The teacher will then explain to all the children that these special possessions must be very carefully looked after.

● In my experience, *teasing* (I am *not* talking about *bullying*) only increases if the perpetrator sees that his victim is upset by it and, even worse, if he knows that his parents have been involved. The best advice to the child is to ignore someone who is teasing him, rather than to get another adult to intervene for him. The child teaser will, more often than not, get bored and go in search of another target. Obviously, a child in a situation where he is being teased needs to be able to talk about what has happened to him, so this is where you and the teacher come in. Both of you can provide him with the comfort and support he needs to enable him to deal with the situation on his own. Ignoring unkind behaviour is a difficult thing to do and requires courage and willpower.

● Children are very fickle with their relationships and if your child is out of favour today, he is very likely to be back in favour tomorrow. Recognise that he may be feeling hurt and lonely, but encourage him to ask to join in with some of the other children and reassure him that C, D and E will soon come back. Again, if the problem remains, it is better to have a quiet word with the teacher – without your child – than to get involved yourself.

DIFFICULT FEELINGS FOR CHILDREN

Examples of difficult feelings include:

● aggression
● frustration
● jealousy
● possessiveness
● fear
● loneliness.

All these feelings are extremely common in children and need to be acknowledged and talked about, not just ignored. Some children may need the help of an adult to be able to express themselves clearly.

Dealing with these feelings in school

In school, all children have a right to feel safe and happy. They should not be subjected to aggression, resulting from others' feelings of frustration, jealousy or possessiveness. One of the teacher's primary aims will be to prevent this kind of disruption in her class. If it occurs, despite her best efforts, she will, most likely, ask for and expect apologies from the parties involved. Sometimes this is sufficient to 'take the heat out of' the situation and settle things relatively amicably. It is really up to the teacher to decide whether a particular incident needs further investigation or whether it can be dealt with as a one-off incident. Serious incidents will be addressed immediately and in such a way as to try to ensure that selfish acts are not repeated. The teacher will try to make sure that she understands – with the help of parents, if necessary – why a particular problem is occurring.

One of the measures she will probably take is to encourage the children involved to talk about the problem. This will help them to work out different, more useful strategies for dealing with their aggressive feelings and for responding to provocative acts.

- What did they do?
- What could they have done instead?
- What will they try to do in the future?

The teacher will also keep a very close eye on the various relationships within her classroom, especially those she has identified as potential problem areas. She may decide to involve the whole class in a discussion so that copycat, undesirable behaviour is seen as disruptive and kindness and consideration is encouraged. Asking the children to imagine the different feelings of the people involved can make the discussion more meaningful and relevant to them.

- Have they ever felt like that?
- When?

Helping feelings of fear and uncertainty

Many new situations are potentially threatening to young children. For many children – and parents – as stated earlier, the first day at school can be a very traumatic experience. Make sure you allow plenty of time to discuss this event and the feelings associated with it (for both of you) in advance of the big day. The more your child knows about what is likely to happen and how both of you are going to cope with the changes, the more comfortable he is likely to feel. It can be helpful to remind him of previous new experiences and how you both managed to cope with these. However, it is probably best to avoid too much discussion on the day itself, when both of you are likely to be feeling particularly vulnerable. Dwelling too much on feelings at this stage can be counter-productive as it can stop children from becoming involved in other activities which might help them to settle more easily.

Helping feelings of sadness and loneliness

Encourage your child to be kind and considerate to others. This will help him to be treated well in return and will make it easier for him to make new friends. Emphasise the importance of joining in.

Helping feelings of aggression, frustration, jealousy and possessiveness

All children have spells of aggressive behaviour. The reasons for this need to be recognised and talked about and children need to be helped to find alternative ways of dealing with these unhelpful feelings and keeping them under control. If your child is aggressive towards others, consider the underlying reasons and try to help him with these. If he becomes the victim of aggression, accept his likely, automatic, aggressive response (however inappropriate), listen to his story, show appropriate levels of sympathy and then consider together alternative ways of dealing with the aggression shown to him. By doing this, you are helping him to realise that certain responses do not solve problems whereas others – such as showing tolerance – may.

There are very many reasons for children's aggressive behaviour. Some children have naturally occurring fiery tempers, while others are much more docile. Some are aggressive much of the time, while others have to be seriously provoked before they retaliate in any way. Aggressive behaviour can often be caused by jealousy, intolerance, frustration or possessiveness. All parents can probably cite instances of aggression which have been sparked off by all these feelings and teachers will be able to confirm this as well. The following case study illustrates an example of aggressive behaviour that was almost certainly caused by frustration.

CASE STUDY

Mark was a bright boy, very bouncy, with a good sense of humour and interested in everything. He had also built up a reputation for being 'naughty'. Mark was very capable of tackling more or less anything that was put in front of him. He was always one of the first to finish any task, but his work was often not very well presented as he had rushed through it and was then distracting and annoying others. Suspecting frustration and boredom, I stepped up his challenges by giving him work that required more thought and effort. Gradually, I noticed a difference in the way Mark behaved towards his peers and in his whole attitude to school. He became enthusiastic about and took pride in his work and was more considerate in his relationship with others.

Otherwise delightful children can often disappoint teachers with their thoughtless behaviour towards their peers. Their behaviour is usually not malicious but arises out of frustration through having work that is too easy. Any child needs to be stretched – not pushed – in order to make life interesting for them. When they have mastered a particular mathematical concept, they need to practise applying that to new situations. When they can form individual letters quite neatly, they need to move on and form those letters into words. When learning to read, they need to be constantly challenged with new words. One way of dealing with children's aggression can be to give them more complicated work to do. Unfortunately, once a child has a 'naughty' label attached, it is very difficult to get rid of this. Far better to try to avoid the situation altogether by keeping children busy and making sure they have enough interesting work, at a suitable level, to be getting on with.

Suggested strategies for dealing with difficult feelings

- *Aggression.* 'Time out' works well, removing the child from the scene for a while and using some diversionary tactic to interest him elsewhere.

- *Frustration.* Recognise the feeling, allow the child to have a break and when you resume, use a calm tone and encouraging language.

- *Possessiveness*. Remind children that sharing can be fun – it gives you a chance to try something different.

- *Jealousy*. Don't try to be too fair – life isn't! – and you are trying to prepare him for 'Life'. Some jealous feelings are inevitable during childhood (and beyond!). Endeavour to make your child see that you understand why he is feeling jealous and that some situations are very hard to accept (for adults as well!), but that jealous feelings are usually rather unhelpful and it is better to try to dispel them by thinking about things he has/does which make him feel good. Make sure that you praise all the kind, positive behaviour your child displays and remind him how lucky you all are, compared with some people around the world.

OTHER COMMON COMPLAINTS ABOUT SCHOOL

Not liking school food

Many children are fussy eaters and will not readily try any new food, automatically assuming they will not like it, which is why most schools try to include food in their menus that is familiar to children. However, as we all know, food that is not made by mother (or father!) at home never tastes as good – 'but you like fish fingers' – 'they're not like the ones we have at home'!

These kinds of reaction are very common at school and usually children are gently encouraged, but not forced, to eat. However, what children drink is very carefully monitored, especially in hot weather, as it is much easier for them to become dehydrated than to come to much harm through not eating a big meal at school. I never cease to be amazed how children seem to get through the day quite happily without eating very much at all. They will eat quickly enough when they become really hungry.

It is, of course, increasingly common for children to opt out of school meals altogether and to go for a packed lunch instead (See Appendix 1, Advice on packed lunches). For many, this works well, although it does put an additional burden on parents, who have to prepare it. There is, however, no doubt that packed lunches can also give rise to problems, when one child has an undoubtedly healthy, but possibly less attractive lunch than the child next to him. If you are prepared to take the time, there are, of course, many ways round this, making all food appealing to your child.

Not wanting to wear school uniform

Usually, the days of uniform wearing come as a relief to parents who no longer have to battle, especially with daughters, over what to wear. There is now only one option. However, some children can resent this and make their parents' lives very difficult in the mornings. Take heart, as soon as children get used to the school routine and see their peers in uniform as well, these adverse feelings should quickly disappear.

Not wanting to go out into the playground

During the first few weeks of a new school term, there are generally a few children who are reluctant to go out into the playground to play. This is usually a combination of a fear of the unknown and concern about having no one to play with. As long as the reluctance is acknowledged and sympathetically dealt with, these fears generally pass quite quickly. Obviously, encouragement to play with others is important but so is the reassuring feeling of having teachers close by.

Children should be allowed to stand back and observe what happens in this new environment for a while if they do not feel immediately ready to join in. Sometimes, some of the more confident children will be able to take some of the shyer ones 'under their wings' and make them feel more comfortable. For others, it can just be a matter of time before they feel secure enough to use the playground with total confidence.

PARENTS' COMPLAINTS AND DIFFICULTIES

● 'I am not being listened to.'

● 'My child is being picked on.'

● 'I am not being told about problems arising with my child.'

Even when you have very carefully chosen your school, there is no guarantee that you and your child will both be happy with it. Sometimes, parents and teachers find that they have a very tricky relationship. Both parties seem to see things very differently and find it very hard to put their points across in ways that are not misunderstood. It can be tempting, under such circumstances, to feel like removing your child from the school. However, unless, things have developed into a serious problem, this is probably unwise, at least without substantial effort to put things right first. Do not forget that you have carefully selected this school for all sorts of reasons and the school will have selected its teaching staff very carefully. Try to see the situation as a temporary setback which should improve with effort on both sides. This book is written specifically to try to avoid such situations by offering suggestions for improving relationships between all parents and teachers. Teachers will act as professionals even when they find certain relationships difficult. Your role is to try to do all you can to improve the situation before giving up on it. If, despite your very best efforts, things do not improve, then is the time to consider going elsewhere.

It is inevitable and actually rather reassuring that different teachers, children and parents find different teachers, children and parents easier to get on with than others. This year may be a more difficult one for you but the next may be particularly good. I am sure teachers try to treat all parents and children the same, but they are human and, as in the rest of their lives, they will react more easily to some than to others. Adults have to relate to many different people in the course of their working and social lives. Children also have to learn to make relationships with others – those who become special friends and those who do not. Having to work with different teachers is very good practice for them.

SUMMARY

- Always listen and accept, but be prepared to challenge your child as well.

- Remember your role is to help your child to learn to cope on his own.

- Allow time for reflection and discussion before giving up on a situation.

4

Responsibilities of Parents and Teachers

Having carefully made your choice, now is the time to think about *your* role in all this. Even when children start full-time school, they are still at home for more than half their waking hours. This point needs to be very firmly borne in mind because it is vital to realise that you still have a very important role to perform and it is not just down to the teacher from now on. Yes, you have chosen the school, yes, you have put your trust in its teachers, yes, you are happy for them to get on with their job of teaching your child, but no, you cannot now opt out completely. In order to get the best from your child's education, you, as well as your child, need to feel comfortable about your relationship with his teacher. It is, of course, fully recognised that many parents now work full-time and this responsibility will sometimes be shared with other family members, nannies and friends. So, . . . realising this.

WHAT DOES THE TEACHER EXPECT FROM YOU?

1.   She needs and will expect your input

Most teachers will also welcome your input if it is given in a helpful way. Young children get the best out of their education when there is a close, working partnership between parents and teachers. This partnership does not mean that parents should try to do the teacher's job or teachers, try to do the parents' job. It is, however, possible to give useful support. Giving your support does not mean that you must agree with everything the teacher does or, indeed, accept it without question. However, having put your trust in the school, you should also put your trust in the teacher. This means believing that she will have good reasons for doing what she is doing and will have the best interests of your child at heart.

Most teachers recognise that you are the expert on your child. You have been living with him for the past four years of his life and you know his innermost thoughts and feelings. You will be the most receptive to his moods. Most will welcome your insight and will value helpful information. They will expect you to be involved in the education of your child but there is a fine line between involvement and interference and it should be recognised that the teacher is ultimately in charge of her classroom – a classroom you have carefully chosen for your child.

2. She will ask you to help your child with his homework

Homework sounds rather grand at this young age but usually means reading or word games initially. You will be asked to feed back information about how your child has found this. This information will help the teacher to assess how various teaching approaches are working with your child. She will expect you to tell her of any specific difficulties or worries that your child has and it will also be very helpful if she can be told (in confidence) about any personal circumstances which could be adversely affecting your child. This is to enable her to be as supportive and understanding as possible.

3. She will ask you to look very carefully at your child's report and to act on this

Individual schools will differ in how often they issue written reports to parents, but when these arrive, they should be very carefully looked at. Most teachers take a great deal of time and trouble to make reports as useful as they can by providing plenty of relevant information. In most schools, gone are the days of statements such as:

- satisfactory progress
- could do better
- very good.

Reports are now generally very detailed and can provide helpful suggestions for improving children's work – some of which you can carry out at home (See Appendix 3, Sample Report). It is vital that you read, carefully digest and try to implement suggestions made in reports, clarifying points with your child's teacher if this proves necessary. It is recognised that some reports may still seem confusing and unhelpful despite the teacher's best endeavours. It is not always easy to get messages across clearly. If, having read a report, there is anything which you do not understand or any issues which concern you, try to ask for clarification as soon as possible. It is far easier for both parties to discuss things when they are fresh in everyone's mind.

4. She will expect you to be interested and involved in your child's school life

It is crucial that both your child and your child's teacher feel that you are interested and involved in your child's school life. This means:

- coming to parents' evenings and other school events – as many as possible – especially those directly involving your child

- reading school letters (particularly about activities and outings) very carefully and acting on them to ensure that your child does not miss out

- replying to notes quickly and responding to specific requests, e.g. for help with school outings, without repeated prompting

- showing that school work which has gone home with a child has been noticed and looked at by removing it from the child's bag or folder.

On occasions, important letters can find their way to the bottom of school bags and folders so it is a good idea to check these every evening!

5. She will expect you to be on time when delivering and collecting your child

The teacher will expect you to deliver your child to school and to pick him up from school on time or to make arrangements for someone else to. Obviously, there will be the odd occasion when things go wrong, but if you regularly put your own needs (e.g. finishing shopping trips, returning late from days out) higher than those of your child at these times, you are sending him the wrong messages. The end of the school day is a time when he really needs you to show interest in him and what he has been doing.

6. She will ask you to make sure that your child is suitably equipped for school

The teacher will expect you to make sure that your child has everything he needs for school and that he is in a fit state for the school day. As a teacher, seeing a yawning child at 9 o'clock in the morning is rather depressing and trying to interest that yawning child is well-nigh impossible. Both teachers and parents can reasonably expect children to be tired at the end of a busy day (some manage to stay as fresh as a daisy, despite the teacher's efforts!), but children cannot get the most out of school if they are always tired, so bedtime needs to be carefully thought about.

7. She will ask you to make sure that you do not send your child to school when he is ill

You will be expected to act responsibly with regard to your child's health and the potential effect this could have on the rest of the class – and the teacher! If he has a heavy cold or a tummy upset, he should not be sent to school as these complaints, although relatively trivial, are very quickly passed on. Teachers tend to build up a fairly high degree of immunity over the years but young children are not so lucky.

As a teacher, trying to cope with a child in the classroom who is clearly ill and should not be in school is not an easy task.

As a parent, I have a lot of sympathy with parents who are trying to assess whether their child's complaints are genuine or not and whether they should be sending them to school. It is very easy to get it wrong! However, it is an area that needs very careful thought – both ways!

The ongoing problem of nits will never be stamped out properly if parents do not regularly check their child's hair, report incidents of infection and deal with these appropriately.

8. She will expect you to name all clothes and everything else that your child brings into school

The teacher will expect all your child's belongings to be clearly named and in school when required. Over the years, I have seen children very upset by not having the correct clothing, unnamed clothing (which means it gets lost) and clothing and shoes that are too small. Teachers have a responsibility to care for their pupils and they will endeavour to do all they can to provide a caring environment and make children feel comfortable, but they cannot provide children with their basic needs for the school day. This is part of the parents' role.

WHAT DOES THE TEACHER EXPECT THE CHILDREN TO BE ABLE TO DO?

Parents obviously have a considerable role to play in helping their children to be ready for school and I include a chapter on this later on. However, the following is a short list of some of the more basic teacher expectations of children when they start school. Obviously, different children develop at different rates and some may well have difficulty in responding to some of these challenges until they are older. However, it will be very helpful for the teacher and good for the morale of your child if he can be encouraged to:

- be independent about going to the loo and washing his hands

- dress and undress himself with the minimum of help – tying shoelaces excepted! (Velcro can be very helpful here!)

- hang up his coat and put his shoes together

- use a knife and fork to eat, having had food cut up if necessary

- recognise his own name

- sit properly in his chair and keep still when asked to

- handle books correctly and carefully

- be used to helping with a variety of tasks, including tidying up

- concentrate for more than a few minutes, i.e. for sufficient time to complete a task

- listen carefully when required to

- be able to share when playing with others in the group.

Helping your child to move on from here

If you have time on your hands and your child is motivated and interested in doing some more formal learning, you could help him with the following:

- Holding a pencil correctly, with the help of a pencil grip if necessary, and writing lower case letters, *not* capitals. (Pencils should be gripped firmly between the thumb and first finger of the hand, with the middle finger acting as a support - most grips are triangular in shape and hold the fingers and thumb in the correct positions.)

- The sounds letters make, not their proper names. (Please note that schools differ in the way they teach letter shapes and sounds, so if you are planning to do some work in this area, get advice from your school before starting. There are many excellent books available.) (see Further Reading).

● Using numbers and mathematical language in practical ways (how many do we need? which has most/least? which is longer/shorter?) *rather than* written sums.

However, the most important skills you can teach him at this stage are how to listen and how to concentrate while encouraging him to ask lots of questions. Children come into school with a wide range of previous experiences and teachers are used to taking them on from where they are.

UNDERSTANDING BASELINE ASSESSMENT

All children are now assessed when they first start school, although the timing of this is currently under review. This is called **Baseline Assessment** and it gives an indication of children's wide range of abilities as they enter school. It is a measure of their knowledge, understanding and abilities at this time, but it is not a test or exam and should not be regarded as such. When teachers are completing this Baseline Assessment for their Reception children, they will be looking at the type of personal and social skills described above as well as looking at children's abilities in other areas, particularly Language and Literacy and Mathematics. Children will not be 'marked down' if they *can't do* things. What they can do will be fully acknowledged and what they *can't do* will be worked on.

If children have the basic skills of listening and concentration and the type of enquiring mind outlined above, they will be in a very good position to start formal learning, even if they have not begun any before. So, please do not feel that you are letting your child down if you do not have time to help him with learning letters and numbers.

WHAT SHOULD YOU EXPECT FROM YOUR CHILD'S TEACHER?

It goes without saying that she should be expected to provide your child with the best education she possibly can. She should do everything in her power to make sure that she understands how to get the very best out of your child.

1.   You should rightly expect to be able to discuss matters with her as they arise.
Teachers should make you feel totally comfortable about raising

difficulties and problems – logistical, emotional or academic. They should be understanding, prepared to have an open discussion and willing to work out strategies for solving any problems with you. Most will be only too glad to do just that. However, feelings of anxiety and worry still remain when arranging meetings of this sort and, as a parent, I can still remember having to take my courage in both hands when raising some issues.

Finding the right time to talk to the teacher
This can sometimes be quite difficult. It is best to try to pick a time when both parent and teacher can feel relaxed. The morning, once children start arriving, is a busy time, especially at the beginning of a new term, when the teacher is having to settle many new children. In addition, once new children have settled in, some teachers like to use this time for one-to-one reading. It is therefore not a good time to be discussing anything other than very simple matters, which can be dealt with immediately. Equally, after school can be a bad time as teachers are tired and may be rushing off to meetings or be dealing with children who have not been collected.

Ask your teacher when it would be most convenient to have a word. You will find that she will have a preferred time for seeing parents. You should not feel that asking to see her constitutes a formal appointment and therefore a very big deal. Some discussions are very straightforward. It is simply much easier logistically for her to arrange discussions in this way.

I found the best time was before school opened. Parents could arrive early with their child or children. At this time, it was possible for another member of staff to look after the children in another classroom while we had a quiet discussion. This way, both parents and teacher felt relaxed in the knowledge that their children were being looked after and were not longing to get home at the end of the day or waiting to be settled in in the morning. By fixing a meeting the following morning or a few days ahead, I had enough time to make the necessary arrangements in order to give parents my undivided attention. There are realistically very few problems that cannot wait a few hours until the next morning. Obviously, in an emergency, teachers should do all they can to help and be flexible.

2. When your child is given homework, you should have the part you are expected to play in this very carefully explained to you

If he is given special work to do to help him with a particular difficulty, you should be put fully in the picture as to why and exactly what he is expected to do. If you are unsure about anything you should feel able to ask for further explanation. If the school or the teacher change their policy on the issuing of homework, you should be told about this and the reasons for it. We often suspended homework in the last week of term, especially the Christmas term. At the end of this busy term, there was so much happening that the children were too tired to be able to cope with homework as well as everything else.

3. You should receive regular reports on your child's progress

These will be in the form of written reports, formal discussions at parents' evenings and informal chats. You should be told at an early stage of any causes for concern. You should also be given the opportunity to ask questions about the teaching of all areas of the curriculum, either through arranged meetings or in informal discussions. The dates for most of these formal meetings will have been worked into the school diary for the term, so it is reasonable to expect plenty of notice of them.

4. You should be told about the organisation of the school day

Schools will differ in the ways they organise their days to allow time for everything in the curriculum and you should be told about this or shown a timetable.

5. You should be kept well informed about school policy

At all stages of your child's schooling, you should be kept well informed about any changes to the school routine or school policy which directly affect you and your child. Schools are continuously updating their procedures and in order to be able to work collaboratively with the school, it is important that you know what these changes are. The school may issue information directly to you or keep you informed via your class teacher.

6. Your teacher should try to be consistent, while allowing some room for flexibility

Ideally, your teacher should show consistency towards discipline and what she expects from the children so that they know exactly where they are. However, if she shows flexibility in her approach to teaching methods this will cater for all children's needs and will allow her time to explore individual children's specific interests.

5

Adapting to School

UNDERSTANDING THE PARENT'S ROLE

Parents and teachers both have a crucial role to play in building up children's confidence and helping them to meet future expectations as they progress through their new school. This chapter identifies some of the approaches parents can adopt while the next outlines some strategies teachers can use. The section is not a list of 'must do's', but is intended to be helpful by giving parents and children aims and goals to be working towards, at their own pace.

All children have different characters and skills. Some have a natural sense of responsibility and have no problem in organising themselves, whereas others find this aspect of life much more difficult. Some have a natural sense of empathy, while others are much more self-centred. Some are starting school at just four, while others are almost a year older. There will inevitably be significant differences in their individual skills. Added to which, most children are susceptible to mood swings and spells of day-dreaming and may be very co-operative and responsible one day, only to be the absolute opposite the next! Do not lose heart! As a parent myself, I am fully aware of the daily constraints in a busy household and, therefore, the difficulties in always implementing these approaches.

Let's picture the scene

It is 8 o'clock in the morning. You have three children aged 7, 5 and 3. Your 3-year-old is crying as he doesn't want to eat breakfast, your 7-year- old is being very slow and is only half-dressed and your 5-year-old is complaining of a sore tummy. There are no other adults in the house and you need to leave for school and work in a quarter of an hour. I am sure you can identify the feelings very well – anger, frustration, worry, to mention just a few! You know you should stick firmly to your 'rules', but you are human and of course you don't. Don't worry about it. This book is not about superheroes, it is about real people and real people don't always have the reserves to deal with every situation as they would like to.

HELPING CHILDREN TO DEVELOP THE RIGHT ATTITUDE TO LEARNING

1. Helping children to ask questions and to listen to explanations

School life is all about asking. Children are always encouraged to ask questions to extend their knowledge and to ask, ask, ask, particularly when they do not understand something. Obviously, to make the most of having asked the question, they need to listen carefully to the answer. Although some children may well feel shy about asking for help in front of the whole class at first, they will gradually feel less intimidated especially if they have had positive reactions to their questions at home. However, if they have experienced negative responses – being told off or ridiculed – this will make the prospect of future asking much more daunting. Children desperately need to ask questions at school so it is very important to build up their confidence to do so. The basic difference between 'home asking' and 'school asking' is that children will need to learn to put up their hand and wait without shouting out, when they want to know something. Some control over questioning in the classroom is essential for the teacher's sanity!

One of the most challenging features of teaching this young age group is to try to answer children's questions in a way which they can readily understand. As children grow, their interest in the world grows too and questions become deeper and more complicated, but teachers will always try to provide explanations which are as simple as possible. They will try to relate any new concepts to things which are familiar to the children and will therefore make sense to them. Involving the children and using human or physical props can often be helpful and is a tried and tested method. It certainly helps them to understand. You may well know the ancient chinese proverb 'we hear – we forget, we see – we remember, we do – we understand'. Never is this truer than with young children.

There are all sorts of ways of actively involving the children. For instance:

- Allowing children with a variety of shoe soles to try to slide along a carpet can provide a very clear demonstration of the issues surrounding friction. Those with smooth leather soles will find it easy whereas those with ridged, rubber ones will find it almost impossible. The children with smooth leather soles may well have experienced slipping on a wet pavement.

- Children can gain a basic understanding of the properties of various materials by comparing items they use every day. Their plastic, shiny mac keeps them dry in the rain. They can find out why their woollen jersey would not do the job as well by pouring water over both (over a water bath, to catch the drips!) and observing what happens. Feeling the heavy, wet jersey and seeing water that has run off the mac in the bath helps them to understand where the water has gone.

As a parent, what can you do?

Encourage your children to ask questions such as:

- how things work
- who is in photographs
- what's for tea
- which book you are going to read
- when you are picking them up.

Try to answer straight away, in simple terms, so that you maintain your child's interest in listening carefully to your answer. With straightforward requests, this is easy, but when faced with a question which could well appear on an exam paper in Physics, this is a little more taxing! Despite these complicated questions often being asked at the most inconvenient and awkward moments (I remember one famous occasion when I was confronted with a 'where do babies come from?' question from my daughter just as we were supposed to be going out for the evening), try to answer immediately (I am sure I failed miserably) in simple terms, leaving the door open for expansion at a later stage if it is necessary to cut the discussion short. Ideally, children should never be made to feel that their endless questioning is a bore, even if after the fifteenth 'why' it can seem that way! Keep reminding yourself that this is a very positive trait in your child and try to recognise his intense desire to find out about burning issues.

Sometimes children ask lots of questions in order to gain attention. It is usually possible to distinguish between this type of questioning and the sort of questioning that stems from a genuine desire to find out. If your child is an attention-seeker, asking lots of questions in order to get his own way, this needs investigating further.

2. Helping children to answer questions and respond to requests

Questions from teachers usually fall into two categories. The first kind are those which ask children about specific things or ask them to contribute to class discussions. The second kind make specific requests, e.g. for taking messages, tidying up or looking after a new pupil. The first kind require verbal answers, whereas the second need practical responses from the children. Teachers will give children encouragement to answer and respond but it is helpful if children are used to both sorts of questions.

As a parent, what can you do?

Once your child has had a chance to wind down from school, show your interest in him by asking him about his day and about his thoughts and feelings, even if his answers are not always very forthcoming. Questions should be of the open-ended kind – those which encourage longer answers, for example:

● 'Tell me what you enjoyed doing today.'

● 'Tell me what the matter is.'

not closed, such as:

● 'Did you enjoy school today?'

to which the answer is really only 'yes' or 'no'. This will encourage your children to be open with you and not to bottle things up inside, especially any problems or unhappiness. To encourage them to answer these questions meaningfully, they need to know that you will always be interested in what they have to say. Try not to answer yourself any questions directed at your children. Gentle prompting can be helpful but avoid the temptation to take over the conversation for them. If children get used to people answering for them, they will learn that they do not have to respond. This does not build confidence or encourage interaction with others. Quite the opposite, it can encourage your child to become shy and withdrawn.

Ask your child to help you in the home – any everyday tasks will do.

If there are others in the family, perhaps he could also help you with looking after them. He may be more willing if he can see that his help will make a real difference to you, that you are really grateful and that he may benefit from your extra attention as a result.

3. Helping children to develop curiosity and an enquiring mind

Children who want to know about things are at an advantage. Their desire to investigate and discover gives them the confidence to ask questions and makes it easier for them to absorb answers. By choosing topics of interest to children, teachers will try to develop this curiosity into a genuinely enquiring mind which will be very helpful to them in their future learning.

As a parent, what can you do?

Watch your child carefully as he grows up. What interests him? What makes him excited? Take up this lead and encourage this interest first before taking him into other areas by letting him see and hear what excites you. When you discover something new, say something like 'I never knew that – that's interesting.' Show him how it is possible for you to use an encyclopaedia to find out something you don't know and let him see you use a dictionary to check spellings. Visit the library together. Computers, the Internet and CD Roms open up all sorts of possibilities for parents and children to have fun 'finding out' together. This can be a genuinely shared experience and one which brings adults and children closer together as they use their knowledge of how the various media work. The important thing is to let your child see that the 'finding out' process is a very positive experience and one to be encouraged.

4. Helping children to be motivated

Teachers are, on the whole, a pretty patient breed but they do want children to try. Young children have a tremendous source of **energy** and if this energy can be directed towards **effort**, they are on the right lines for success. Teachers will try to do everything they can to help and support children and to encourage them to try and try again, especially when they are finding something hard.

As a parent, what can you do?

Encourage your child to persevere. Choose something that he is interested in and praise him when he manages something new totally on his own. For instance, if he is fond of Lego, see if he can make something without help from you. (The added incentive being that he can then have it to play with much earlier than if you were to help him, as you are not free until after tea.) Help him to accomplish new tasks in achievable steps so that he is always experiencing success and progress through perseverance. This will help him to realise that he can do new things, even when he thinks he can't.

5.   Helping children to be enthusiastic

One of the truly delightful things about being a teacher of very young children is their infectious enthusiasm and natural zest for life. I remember growing an amaryllis in the classroom one year and the excitement generated as a result is something I shall never forget. The children were involved in planting the dead-looking, very uninteresting bulb with its worm-like roots and they would not go home until they had lovingly watered it. Their patience was soon rewarded as strong green leaves appeared, together with the enormous stem, growing substantially almost every day. As the buds appeared – we had four – the anticipation heightened and when these actually flowered, they could barely contain their excitement. How rewarding!

Enthusiasm is something that needs to be carefully nurtured both at home and at school. Teachers will do everything they can to capitalise on this spontaneous enthusiasm by trying to provide plenty of original and exciting opportunities in the classroom.

As a parent, what can you do?

Let your children see you showing enthusiasm for things. Such are the pressures of day-to-day life these days that we all too often forget to observe and enjoy what is going on around us. It doesn't matter what you are enthusiastic about, but children do need to see you finding things really exciting or beautiful or moving. I went on a short holiday with my husband to Scotland one October. The weather was beautiful and the trees were looking quite magnificent in all their autumn colours. As we drove round, I had to keep stopping for a good look – round every corner, the colours were even more spectacular. My natural enthusiasm was certainly in very good working order and I have a room full of photographs to prove it! I fear that my family are now too old and too cynical to appreciate my childlike excitement! However, no such worries with young children of this age – make the most of it!

6.   Helping children towards independence

Children in school are at a disadvantage if they are unable to do basic tasks for themselves, such as dressing and undressing, changing shoes, going to the loo efficiently and so on. Always having to have help from the teacher results in feelings of inferiority and being different, neither of which are conducive to building confidence in this new environment. In contrast, an ability to do things for themselves helps children to feel in control.

As a parent, what can you do?

Obviously, all children are different. Some are fiercely independent from a very early age, desperate to do everything for themselves, while others are much more reliant on adult help. Those who find it more difficult to get their act together need special encouragement. Try to build up your child's independence when you are not under pressure to get somewhere. Perhaps he could help you to lay the table (which will help to develop his counting and matching skills) or put away the washed clothes (sorting skills here as well). Make sure he helps to tidy up his room at the end of the day and give him jobs to do to help you around the house.

Encouraging him to do things for himself in this way will help when it comes to getting himself organised for school and also looking after himself at school. On school days, try to leave plenty of time for your child to dress himself in the morning, only offering help if this really becomes essential. Try not to respond to his every plea for help, offering praise instead when he manages to do it for himself.

7.   Helping children to concentrate on a task for a reasonable length of time

Children need to be able to concentrate carefully on what the teacher is saying and doing in order to get the most out of their lessons and to be able to fully understand what the teacher is teaching them. If children can focus their attention on the task in hand, they are at an advantage when it comes to learning new concepts and skills. I always used to talk about 'switching brains on' and this seemed to help.

As a parent, what can you do?

Encourage greater concentration by playing games involving memory, e.g. 'I went shopping and I bought. . .' or 'matching pairs' card games. Identify a new skill that your child is keen to learn e.g. sewing and take some time to teach him. Give him plenty of encouragement and praise him when he manages to increase his periods of concentration, especially when he manages to complete what he set out to do.

CASE STUDY

Sarah found it difficult to settle down to writing and maths work. She was always day-dreaming and losing the thread of what was going on. When questioned, she found it hard to answer. She couldn't sit still and was always fidgeting with her pencil. Sarah's concentration span for this type of work was very limited. By contrast, when she was playing with construction material, Sarah's whole attitude changed as she became completely absorbed in her make-believe play, creating something from nothing. She was clearly capable of concentrating for quite some time on this task. Once this was pointed out and praised, Sarah was able to recognise and begin to apply that concentration to tasks which, for her, were harder. Her confidence gradually grew and her other work improved accordingly.

HELPING CHILDREN TO MAKE FRIENDS

1. Helping children to join in

It is all too easy for some children to feel 'left out' at the beginning of a new school year. More outgoing characters in the class can tend to take over, both in discussions and in games, making it easy for the quieter ones to be overlooked. Teachers will do all they can to stop this happening but it will help your child quite enormously if he is prepared to have a go at everything even if he finds it difficult. This will help to ensure that he is included and encouraged and will hopefully avoid the possibility of him being ignored by some of his peers.

As a parent, what can you do?

Make sure you include your child in discussions and let him speak for himself when asked questions by other children and adults. Encourage him to accept invitations away from his home. Do not force, but apply some pressure to ensure that he does not miss out on opportunities for doing something different and exciting. Shyness can best be overcome by suggesting that he goes with a friend. Play games involving active participation and join in yourself. Learn new songs and rhymes together.

Play 'I Spy' and other games involving guesswork. Tell a 'family' story – each member of the family adding another sentence. Encourage new friendships.

2.   Helping children to be aware

The school day is a very busy one and in order to gain the maximum benefit from it, children need to be alert and receptive to what is going on around them.

- What does that bell mean?
- What must we do before lunch?
- Why is my friend upset?

Teachers are only too aware of the need for eyes in the back of their heads. Any teacher will tell you how she counts children every few minutes when out of school on trips, how she watches like a hawk when children are playing in the playground and how she constantly reviews the dynamics of her classroom layout. Children need to be able to imagine potential dangers and they have a lot to learn from teachers on the subject of being aware.

As a parent, what can you do?

Talk to your child as you go about your daily tasks, point things out to him and while encouraging him to use all his senses, generally interest him in things in order to help to make him more aware of the world around him. This is important because a child who is in a dream world is potentially at risk all the time, even when walking from room to room in his own home! If a child is to grow up understanding people and the world, he has to become aware of what is going on around him. There is no incentive to find out about how the world works unless you find things that interest you and it is not possible to relate to people unless you are aware of some of the things that make them tick.

3.   Helping children to communicate clearly

Part of the teacher's job is to assess what her children need and to give them help and support. If her pupils are upset, she will try her best to solve the problem. However, some communication from the individual child is necessary if she is to identify his needs correctly. Guesswork is not always effective and can result in frustration all round. In addition, children need to be able to talk to each other in order to develop friendships at school.

CASE STUDY

Some children find it very difficult to communicate directly with those they do not feel completely comfortable with. Teachers may well fall into this category when children first start school. Katie was a very quiet little girl at first and it was impossible to get her to speak up at all in front of the class. She obviously found this very threatening and despite being given lots of encouragement to speak, remained firmly silent. There had to be another way of releasing her communication skills.

We often set up a corner of the classroom as a role-play area of some kind where the children could play freely. One afternoon, we set up this area as a mini schoolroom. Children were allowed to come and go at will and Katie soon investigated the area along with many other children. There were two blackboards and chalk, a 'writing table' with pens and paper and a 'reading table' with several easy readers spread out on it. As we watched discreetly from a distance, we could see the children explore the various areas and hear them assuming the different roles of teacher and pupil.

Katie, who was very reluctant to read her book to us, read it quite happily to her friends. She also astounded us with her confidence, becoming quite bossy and demanding as a teacher! In this 'released' environment, Katie felt totally comfortable and quite happy about speaking out clearly. We subsequently noticed that if we took part as pupils in the role-play, Katie would get so excited that she would sometimes forget who she was talking to and talk to us as well. This kind of non-threatening play was clearly the way forward when encouraging Katie to feel more comfortable about showing her true colours in more formal situations.

As a parent, what can you do?
Talk to your child, read with him and have discussions with him. Encourage him to give you feedback on how his day has gone. Use

different ways of saying things and asking things in order to help him to develop his growing vocabulary. If he uses incorrect grammar, for example:

- I 'sawed' for I 'saw'
- the bus 'goed' for the bus 'went'

repeat his words correctly, but without making a big fuss about it. In this way, your child will gradually absorb the information without feeling criticised.

4. Helping children to say sorry

We all make mistakes and children are no exception. Most problems that occur in the classroom are not really vindictive but are caused by a lack of thought. A child's work gets spoilt because their hand is jogged by someone not looking where they are going, or someone gets hurt because play gets too rough. However accidents happen, it is very important that children are able and willing to say sorry. Any anger felt as a result of such accidents disappears if those who are 'wronged' receive an apology. The incident can then be quickly forgotten. (Serious cases of bullying or any other anti-social behaviour must obviously be dealt with by discussion between all parties.)

As a parent, what can you do?

Make sure your child understands what is expected of him if he has been thoughtless or caused someone pain or distress. It is important that he experiences you apologising too, be it to him or to other members of the family or to friends. Having apologised, he should be allowed to forget the incident and should not have it 'held over him' for long periods of time.

5. Helping children to share and mix well with other children

The Reception classroom provides a tempting environment for young children and the toys and games in it are often in great demand. There will always be enough activities to keep the children occupied, but children won't always be able to have the toy they want precisely when they want it. Inevitably, this means that they will have to share. To make the most of having to share, children need to be able to mix well with others so that they can develop a 'group game'.

As a parent, what can you do?

If you have more than one child in your family, encourage them to share their toys and games and to play together. Obviously, it is important for each child to have his own possessions as well but there are plenty of things which can be shared. If your child is an 'only', try to ensure that you invite other children to your home so that your child gets used to playing with others, co-operating and having to share. Try to make sharing a positive experience by making yourself equally available to all family members. If children think that sharing gives them a poor deal, they will be less inclined to try it.

HELPING CHILDREN TO GET ON WITH THEIR TEACHER

1. Helping children to develop a clear understanding of acceptable and unacceptable behaviour

The distinction between acceptable and unacceptable behaviour is very well defined in schools and teachers work to strict guidelines. Each teacher will have her own interpretation of these but basically, they will make pretty good sense. No will mean . . .no!

As a parent, what can you do?

Make sure your child is given very clear guidelines about acceptable behaviour – guidelines which ideally do not alter according to the time of day! An initial warning in the form of a firm reminder that something is unacceptable is a good idea, but allowing children to 'get away with it' many times if they persist, is not. At the end of a long, hard day, it is so much easier not to argue and haven't we all fallen into this trap and taken the easy option! The trouble is that it makes it very difficult to re-establish what is acceptable at a later stage. In addition, children will not grow up to respect adults who frequently let their children get the better of them.

In a calm moment, give specific examples of each type of behaviour, making sure children understand the difference. They need to appreciate the reasons for what you are saying and why their behaviour might be considered anti-social. As far as possible, children should be able to rely on their parents to teach them what is acceptable and what is not.

Allowing for the odd occasions when emotions get the better of you, if you apply your own common sense to the subject and stick firmly to what you decide, your child should find it relatively easy to make the minor adjustments to his understanding of what is allowed when he transfers from home to school.

2. Helping children to abide by rules and understand boundaries

Boundaries and rules are imposed quite naturally in a school environment – that is part of what school is all about. However, when children first start school, they need to be taken through these so that they fully understand what the rules are and why they are there. For example:

- No running in the corridors because you could bump into people and knock them over.
- No talking when the teacher is talking because it is bad manners.

As a parent, what can you do?

Children need to know where they are. They must be set very clear and logical boundaries and the reasons for these should be very clearly explained to them. Children almost always try to push out these boundaries further and further so you will find it easier if you have a very clear idea of where you are coming from and why. The more logical your arguments can be, the better, because it is much harder to argue against a totally logical statement – even for children! For example:

- Bedtime will be at 7 o'clock because you get grumpy and tearful if you go to bed later than this.
- You cannot go out into the lane because cars come along there and you could get knocked over.

3. Helping children to use their common sense

In order for children to be able to know what is sensible and what is not and why, they need to have experienced a wide range of situations and to have had a certain degree of freedom to experiment for themselves. All children need to use their common sense in order to stop them from being upset by doing something silly. In school, they will obviously be cautioned about potentially dangerous, new situations, but they do need to think for themselves as well.

As a parent, what can you do?

Try not to wrap your children in cotton wool, by which I mean, do not protect them to such an extent that they never have to think for themselves. They should obviously not be exposed to unnecessary danger, but finding a table wobbly when they attempt to stand on it or stubbing a toe because they are not looking where they are going are salutary lessons.

4. Helping children to tell the truth and be aware of right and wrong

It is important for children to know the difference between right and wrong. If they have done something wrong they should realise that they have to put things right as best they can. This means owning up and apologising. At school, 'honesty is the best policy' is a very useful maxim to employ. No teacher will hold a misdemeanour against a child for very long if they own up and apologise. In contrast, most teachers will have experienced the frustration of not being able to get to the bottom of an incident because no child will own up and nothing can be proved. It is very easy, in those circumstances, to get into a position where the only thing to do is to punish the whole class, even though you are pretty sure who the culprit is. This is obviously an unsatisfactory position.

As a parent, what can you do?

Encourage your children to tell the truth. Children need to be taught about right and wrong by giving them specific examples from their own experience. They should understand that it is wrong to take things, or interfere with/destroy things which do not belong to them unless they have been given permission. Involve them in your explanations by asking them why they think this should be so. How would they feel if their precious things were taken by someone else? Very often, at this young age, the temptation to pocket a few Lego bricks or a model car stems from a wish to investigate and play further, not from a true desire to possess. However, the line between 'borrowing' and stealing is a very fine one and this sort of behaviour does need to be discouraged before it becomes a habit. Issue praise when your child owns up without being asked to. Don't lie yourself and make sure that telling the truth is always rated highly in your family.

5. Helping children to have good manners

Teachers like children to be polite and considerate. They expect them to say 'please' and 'thank you' when asking for and receiving what they want and to say 'sorry' when they inadvertently hurt someone, either physically or mentally. They are asked to put up their hands and wait when they want to ask a question (having had this explained to them). When having lunch, it is a pleasure to find children who know how to sit properly, eat nicely and can handle a knife and fork correctly. It is also good to see children who can blow their runny noses rather than sniffing! Children also need to know that it is bad manners to push and shove or to talk when others are talking.

As a parent, what can you do?

Some of these manners are easier to instil in children than others. If you make sure that you say 'please', 'thank you' and 'sorry' in circumstances where you would expect your child to, he will, hopefully, quickly pick up the habit without too much reminding from you. It is up to the teacher to insist on hand-raising. If she ignores the child who shouts out and turns her attention to the child who puts up his hand, children will quickly learn what is expected. The issues surrounding sitting and eating nicely are more difficult to learn and require lots of demonstration, practice, encouragement and praise when children are mastering these skills.

Holding knives and forks correctly is just as important as holding a pencil correctly. Many parents and teachers spend a great deal of time showing children how to hold a pencil correctly. They will place children's fingers on the pencil so that writing feels comfortable and easy and continue to do this at regular intervals whenever children slip back to their old (incorrect) ways. Similar effort is needed when trying to get children to hold knives and forks correctly. They need to be shown how to do it and constantly reminded and re-shown when they revert to bad habits.

Making sure that seat heights are correct for the table height will discourage children from kneeling on their chairs or tipping them backwards. Reminding them of what can happen if they don't sit properly can also be helpful!

If you can have family meals together, or at least, sit down with your children while they eat, it will be easier to keep an eye on and therefore encourage good manners.

Blowing noses is another area that needs specific instruction and plenty of practice. Give your child plenty of tissues and show him how to blow. Whenever he has a runny nose, try to dissuade him from sniffing and encourage him to blow, resisting the temptation to wipe it for him (if you can bear to!).

Talking in general terms about behaviour which is polite and impolite will help him to understand the difference and why he should be striving for the former.

6. Helping children to develop a responsibility for their own possessions

If children have been taught how to hang up their clothes, put shoes away and keep all their other belongings together so they don't get lost, it will be enormously helpful to them and to their teacher. Even in a relatively small class of Reception age children, it is very easy for children to mislay their possessions if they don't understand the need to keep them carefully. Children should be encouraged to take an active role in looking after themselves as early as possible.

As a parent, what can you do?

Obviously, while children are still young, they will need your support and assistance in looking after their own things. However, it is a good idea to let them take on as much responsibility for themselves as they can, from the earliest age. Try to give your child his own space for keeping his clothes, toys and books so that he can feel proud of them and therefore have a vested interest in looking after them carefully. Give lots of encouragement by telling him that you would like him to look after his own possessions both at home and at school so that they do not get spoilt.

Make sure he knows what he needs to take to school and make sure you know if there are special things he needs on particular days. You could perhaps make a chart together, showing days of the week with pictures of what needs to be taken. If possible, stop for a minute before you leave for school to let him think about what he needs and to get anything he has forgotten. If you arrive at school to discover something has been forgotten, do not make your child feel he is to blame, but share the responsibility with him, saying you must both try to remember. If he manages to remind you about something you have forgotten, this will give him a tremendous sense of achievement.

6

Retaining Home Links

This chapter identifies how teachers can develop the 'home' approach that children have grown used to. In a busy Reception classroom, it is very easy for a teacher's best intentions and plans to be completely taken over by the constant demands of these young children. Picture the scene. . .

It is time to go home. The teacher wants to end the day with a story. However, she is still trying to make sure that everyone has been to the loo, has put on the right coat (the right way out!), has the right reading book in the right folder to go in the right school bag. She has several laces to re-tie. She has to make sure she hands out a letter to all the parents. She has to remember to tell Mrs A about . . . and has to remind Mr B about. . . . One of the children is crying because he can't find his gloves, another is asking her a series of questions, a third is trying to show her his special book from home which he has just remembered about.

Talk about Joyce Grenfell! Even she might find her serene manner under pressure! What should the teacher do? Resign tomorrow?! Of course not . . . but she could perhaps improve her organisation and allow more time for winding down the school day. By providing a quiet time at the end of the day, she could send the children home feeling calm and leave herself feeling more in control.

WHAT DO CHILDREN NEED THEIR NEW TEACHER TO DO?

They need her to make school an exciting and happy place where they can rely on her support to build up their self-esteem and to encourage and help them with the learning process.

CREATING A SUCCESSFUL WORKING ENVIRONMENT

1. Continuing to provide children with plenty of attention

Your child has grown up with constant attention of varying kinds as his needs have changed over the years – from routine feeding and cleaning to interested responses to his never-ending demands. It has not always been possible to give him your immediate and undivided attention but he knows that he can rely on you to be there to listen to him, to comfort him and to help him when he needs it. He has come to expect that if he has an urgent problem, you will put his needs first. He should also have learnt that others in the family – or indeed you – need to have priority on other occasions. If he is part of a larger family, he should be appreciating 'special time' for him while also allowing 'special time' for each of his other siblings. It is important that all children receive plenty of attention and vital that both 'good' and 'bad' behaviour are rewarded with attention in the same way. If this does not happen and 'good' behaviour is ignored, the incentive to be 'bad' is increased.

How can your teacher develop this approach?

At school, children should continue to receive careful attention but as they are now in classes of several pupils, that attention will inevitably be somewhat less intense. However, when children need one-to-one attention, they should receive it (maybe not immediately) and they should hopefully feel confident enough to seek it. Every teacher will value the need for special attention for each child at specific times during the school day, for example during one-to-one reading or discussion times. On other occasions, urgent matters should still be dealt with immediately, but if the matter can wait, your teacher should be encouraging the children to become more independent by inviting them to try for themselves. Some pupils are very demanding of the teacher's time and it is then horribly easy to ignore those who are quiet and cause no trouble. This needs to be avoided.

Ideally, what will actually happen in the classroom?

The teacher will spend a lot of time talking individually to all the children in her class as she gets to know them. She will read individually with your child several times during the week. She will ask him direct questions as part of the group discussions. She will offer him individual help during exercises and written work and make sure that he understands what he is doing.

2. Avoiding subjecting children to too much pressure

Children respond well to encouragement and praise. Some need a well-meaning, gentle push as well but not, at this tender age, too much pressure. However, you want them to do well and it is easy to fall into the pressure trap which is liable to switch children off without meaning to. When tempted to pressurise your child into working very hard academically, it is important to remember that he must also have time to do things which help him to develop as a whole person and time to do nothing at all!

How can your teacher develop this approach?

When children first start school, they need to be taught new concepts in a way they can readily understand because they have had some direct knowledge and experience of what is being put across. Learning must be enjoyable and children must want to learn, if they are to get anywhere. Some pushing is necessary, but too much pressure can have a very detrimental effect. Children need to increase their ability to concentrate, to learn to work constructively with others and to be stretched in such a way that encourages them to use their brains to the full but does not leave them floundering. By placing the emphasis on effort, rather than achievement, teachers can send the right messages to their children. It is important that children try hard but they should not be penalised for failing to achieve excellent results immediately.

3. Continuing to offer plenty of help and support

Parents help their children with lots of different things as they grow up and children need to be able to rely on that help in order to develop the confidence to try things for themselves.

How can your teacher develop this approach?

Similarly, children need to feel their teachers will support and help them. However, it is also important that teachers encourage independence as children need to be able to do more for themselves as they grow up if they are to feel good about themselves. A careful balance between help and support and encouraging independence will help to develop self-esteem and build confidence.

4. Continuing to offer explanations

As your child has grown up, he has had to rely on you for explanations about what things mean. Without thinking you will have told him the word for the picture he is looking at, be it a cat or an aeroplane. You will probably also have offered some simple explanation about what that is or what it does. While speaking to your child, it will be very obvious, by his expression, if he has not understood something and you will then automatically clarify it for him. Thus his first knowledge of the world comes from you.

How can your teacher develop this approach?

She can make sure that she explains words and phrases that the children may not have met as yet. She needs to use very simple explanations, possibly illustrating the word or words in a simple sentence. For example, 'line up' means children stand one behind the other in a long line.

5.   Continuing to encourage children

In the first few years of his life, your child has received encouragement at all the major steps in his development – encouragement to smile, to laugh, to hold things, to crawl, to walk, to talk, to use his potty, to clean his teeth and so on. He has grown used to this as a way of helping him to tackle something new and as an incentive to learn how to do it.

How can your teacher develop this approach?

Your teacher needs to be optimistic about each child's performance and should continue to use encouragement daily as a very useful tool for helping children to persevere with anything new which they are finding difficult.

Ideally, what will actually happen in the classroom?

When children are finding something difficult, the teacher will offer help. She will try to use positive, encouraging remarks such as:

● 'That's much better, especially your letter m's.'
● 'You have written all those numbers correctly.'

rather than negative ones such as:

● 'That is still messy'
● 'You are still writing number 3 back to front.'

She will try to put learning into child-friendly contexts which will develop the children's interests, therefore encouraging them to want to learn.

6. Remaining available to the children

Your child will have grown up knowing what 'available' means in your household. It will obviously depend on parents' work commitments, other siblings in the family and so on. You will have worked out how to keep a balance between all these things and fit in everything that you have to do. You will have adopted a lifestyle which works well for you, be it sharing meals together, travel times together, making the most of grandparents or any other magical combination. You may well know the children's story – *Not Now Bernard* by David McKee – (Random House). This book tells the unhappy tale of a young boy, unable to get through to his parents as they are always too busy. He is eaten by a monster while his parents remain blissfully unaware and continue their 'not now' relationship with the monster! This is obviously an extreme story but it does illustrate a point. Children need you to be available to them – not all the time but they do need you and they need to know when they can 'have' you.

How can your teacher develop this approach?

Children have a captive teacher when in the classroom and will always find that their teacher is available when they first start school, although not always in a one-to-one relationship.

7. Providing children with a safe and secure environment

Your child has grown up in the small, secure environment of his home. As yet, he does not have much knowledge of the big, bad world outside. He needs to feel safe in this strange new environment and to be sure that this new place will not be a threat to him. Home has been the comfortable, safe place up to now and school must be an extension of this, while also allowing him a degree of freedom. Your child needs protecting but he also needs to be allowed to grow up.

I sympathise greatly with parents who are becoming increasingly concerned about allowing their young children the freedom to do anything on their own. It is very difficult not to be influenced by the horrific news stories that appear from time to time. However, if children are not given a certain degree of freedom once they are old enough to go to full-time school, they will become frustrated and will not be able to judge for themselves what is safe and what is dangerous. As parents, we have to make it possible for them to do this, however difficult we may find it, by teaching, explaining, warning and then, to a certain extent, trusting. It gets no easier as children get older. They are then exposed to other dangers in the form of drug abuse, dangerous driving and so on.

How can your teacher develop this approach?
She needs to be welcoming and friendly and to make this new school environment for your child as appealing as possible. She also needs to reassure you, as a parent, that security arrangements are adequate and that she will warn the children of potential hazards within school and when they go off site. She should leave you feeling comfortable that your child will be well looked after and that there is a sensible balance between protection and freedom.

8.   Providing quiet times for rest and relaxation
As adults, we recognise the need for times of rest as well as times of exertion and frenzied activity. At the end of a hard day, we need to relax – reading, listening to music, watching television or, indeed, doing nothing at all. We also need time together with loved ones and friends and time alone: time together for talking and playing games – time alone for our own thoughts.

Children are no different and also need their space and time for resting. In a world now so full of opportunities, it is all too easy to become wrapped up in the never-ending whirl of activities after school. When considering the various options for your child, you will have endeavoured to strike a good balance so that your child does not become over-tired.

How can your teacher develop this approach?
The school day is a very busy one and the teacher needs to make sure she allows time for quietly looking at books, listening to stories or listening to music. Children are using their brains very actively during the day and they need to be able to unwind, 'switch brains off' and relax. The teacher needs to explain what 'peace' means and endeavour to create it in her classroom at least once a day!

MAKING SCHOOL EXCITING AND FUN

1.   Making children happy
We all want our children to be happy. We have seen how quickly school assumes an important role in the life of your child and therefore it is essential that school, as well as the home, is seen as a happy place.

How can your teacher develop this approach?

School should be, and can very easily be, a happy place. Teachers have a vested interest in making it a happy place. If their children are happy, they will be happy. Teachers are dedicated to doing a good job and who does a good job if they are miserable?

Ideally, what will actually happen in the classroom?

Teachers will always try to be positive and in a good mood and will be very aware of how important this is. Being greeted by a friendly, smiling face works wonders for parents and children. It immediately helps to make them feel welcome, happy and wanted. In contrast, being met by a teacher in a bad mood will not bring out the best in any parent or child.

Teaching is a very public job which is one reason why it is so exhausting. It is not possible to run away and hide if you have a headache or are worried about an issue out of school. The teacher in a Reception class cannot pretend to be deep in her computer thoughts if she doesn't want to speak to anyone. She has to face a class full of children and what is more, look cheerful about it. She has to put herself very firmly last and concentrate fully on trying to make her children both happy about and interested in what she is trying to teach them. Rest assured, your teacher will be trying her very best!

2.   Providing children with opportunities for spontaneity

Young children are very spontaneous. If they are frustrated or angry, they will hit out or shout; if they hurt themselves, they will scream. When they see a muddy puddle, their first thought (for most) is to jump into it. They do not have any adult reserve and will not be put off by the consequence of wet feet, muddy trousers and a displeased parent. As they grow older, some of that spontaneity goes as they develop more reason and, somewhat sadly, a more realistic view of life. However, it is still very important to make sure that children have opportunities to explore freely, make a mess and be noisy.

How can your teacher develop this approach?

Inevitably, school must be more formally organised than the home environment. To have fifteen to thirty four- and five-year-olds doing exactly as they please in the classroom would quickly result in chaos. How, then, can the teacher create this order while still giving a degree of spontaneity? The secret lies in a flexible approach.

Ideally, what will actually happen in the classroom?

There are areas of the school curriculum where formal work has to be completed in a set pattern. For instance, it is essential for children to learn how to read, write and manipulate numbers and this requires lots of repetition and practice. However, when working on other areas of the curriculum, it is possible to think about concepts and ideas in a number of contexts, encouraging spontaneity by allowing time for concentrating on the children's interests and ideas as well as the teacher's. Hopefully, the teacher in a Reception classroom will always have time to pursue a 'sideline' to the discussion which is of interest to a child. Here are a few examples:

- When learning about materials, we concentrated on the story of the 'Three Little Pigs'. Half-way through the discussion, one of the children said 'I wonder what it's like to try to build a house out of twigs?' Luckily, we had the time and the opportunity to go out into the playground to collect some sticks and we all had a go. It's not very easy!!

- In the middle of a lesson when the children had been sitting still and listening for a while, I quite often used to give them a minute's 'fidget time'. This meant jumping up and down and wriggling around, usually accompanied by whoops of delight. It was certainly an opportunity for making a noise but as it was only a minute, the effects on anyone else were not too disastrous and the results for me and my children's concentration were miraculous.

- Painting is often associated with mess. It is, however, quite possible to direct that mess so that beautiful results are produced. If you watch children after they have been directed in this way, their natural – and spontaneous – reaction at the end of their task will be to use the lovely gooey stuff to paint all over their hands. Most of the mess can be removed onto paper by encouraging them to do hand-prints and no permanent damage is done.

3. Continuing to make the learning process fun

The early discoveries that children make are all through play. Play is fun. Every day, the young child finds out more and more by his own investigations. He is helped in this learning by his parents and other adults who look after him. They will have offered explanations and help as and when this has been necessary. Largely, though, in the first few years of his life, your child will have been in charge of his own learning and he has been having fun.

How can your teacher develop this approach?

Formal schooling is sometimes visualised as just that – rows of desks and a strict teacher in front of the class, reminiscent of Victorian times. Though schools differ in how formal their approach is, none are quite like that! Most will offer at least some time for free choice or play so that your child has some opportunities to continue his investigative learning. At other times, it is the responsibility of the teacher to deliver all areas of the curriculum in an exciting way by actively involving her children in the learning process. Having a well-organised class, where everything is to hand, is important, as is having a classroom environment which is suitably stimulating.

As mentioned before, the key to making learning fun at this age is to structure it within topics (e.g. myself, houses, pets) which the children can understand because they have actually had related experiences. By starting on familiar ground, new territory can quickly be introduced as the teacher already has the children's interest and attention. This way, fun still features strongly in the learning process at the same time as stretching the children.

Children enjoy jokes and if teachers can incorporate these into their teaching, they are guaranteed a captive audience. Gentle teasing can also make the learning process fun – emphasis on the 'gentle'. Always remember – as my children have been told on many occasions – teasing (not bullying) is a sign of affection!

4. Continuing to issue challenges for them to respond to

Children need to have a challenge. They all need to be stretched at their own level and will have been, as you have gradually asked them to take on more responsibility for their own lives. Many everyday and routine activities can be made into challenges. These activities can be made more interesting by setting targets and giving plenty of praise, for example:

- Today can you put on your coat by yourself?
- Can you tidy away your toys by the time I count to twenty?

Challenges are also set during activities outside the home, for example:

- swimming

- music lessons
- Cubs/Brownies
- football
- bicycling

or indeed, new activities within it, for example:

- cooking
- reading
- computer games

and so on. All these give your children something to aim for and a tremendous sense of achievement once that challenge has been conquered.

How can your teacher develop this approach?
She will be providing children with a series of challenges, both in their formal academic work and in their personal and social development. Children have to learn how to concentrate for longer periods, to share, to become more independent and to cope with an enormous number of extra challenges that arise as they go through their school life. In their formal work, new challenges are set every day as children learn more and more complicated things.

5.   Continuing to inspire them
You have given your child much support during his learning and development so far. He has come to rely on you to show him exciting new things by taking him to new places at weekends and during holidays. All these experiences have helped him to develop into a rounded individual who is excited by and interested in making new discoveries.

How can your teacher develop this approach?
She needs to impart information in such a way that children are motivated and continue to find discovery a pleasure and not a chore. When she is aware of her class becoming restless, she needs to feel confident about changing tack and trying another way of keeping the children's interest and concentration.

Ideally, what will actually happen in the classroom?
Very often, long periods of listening are a mistake for this very young

age group. Most teachers will alternate periods of listening with periods of active participation from the children. For example:

- When we were looking at castles as a topic, we involved all the children in a short role-play, dressing them all up as different characters from a medieval castle.

- When children were attempting to learn the shapes of letters of the alphabet, we found it useful to ask them to write the letters in the air or in dry sand at the same time as saying their sounds.

- When looking at fruit and vegetables, children were encouraged to smell and taste the different ones as well as looking at the colours and shapes. They also felt the texture and looked at the stones and seeds while listening to explanations.

Careful use of all five senses – sight, touch, smell, hearing and taste – is a valuable aid to reinforce learning.

6.　Allowing children time to develop their imaginations

Young children grow up listening to fairy stories and are naturally imaginative in the earliest games they play. It is, however, all too easy for children to lose out on imaginative play once they start school and have all sorts of other pressures and demands on their time. In addition, as children grow older, most become more and more involved with characters in computer games and on television. Inevitably, games then become copycat versions of these characters' antics, rather than games which are invented and show true imagination. However diligent you are as a parent, resisting the attraction of these programmes, it is very difficult for you and your child not to become involved when they are the talk of the playground. It is therefore very important that your teacher sees school as a place where imaginative play is positively encouraged.

How can your teacher develop this approach?

Your teacher should encourage pupils to use their imagination at every opportunity. Children need to be able to use their imaginations in order to be creative in art, music and language skills. They also need a good imagination for creative story-writing.

Ideally, what will actually happen in the classroom?

Imaginative play can be encouraged through the use of a home corner set up in a variety of ways. Many Reception classes in school have an area they can set up in this way and, indeed, many have a corner permanently dedicated to this purpose. With the addition of a screen of some kind, together with a wide variety of simple props, the area can be transformed into anything from a garden centre to a space rocket, with endless opportunities for imaginative role-play.

Encouraging children to be creative in art, music and language is a vital part of the curriculum. Often, children will be asked to move around to **music**. Sometimes, it is necessary to direct these movements specifically, but when children are asked to move freely, their imagination comes into play. The same happens with **art** work. The more imaginative a child is, the more interesting the result will be. The children will also be encouraged to use their imaginations when making up class **stories** together or when thinking of different endings to well-known stories. Closing the eyes and sitting still, in silence, for a few minutes is a good way of encouraging young minds to be imaginative.

7.   Offering incentives in the form of rewards and privileges

When children are growing up as part of a family, they need to feel they are important individuals within that family. The eldest child needs to act in a more responsible way when new members arrive and he needs encouragement to do this. He knows that you will allow him to have certain privileges over the younger members if he demonstrates this extra responsibility. This might be going to bed later, having more pocket money or – when my children were growing up – staying up for grown-up supper!

How can your teacher develop this approach?

Children in the same class at school are obviously the same age so they are all expected to behave sensibly. However, it is important to keep issuing incentives for children and privileges and rewards for good behaviour, kindness and hard (not necessarily neat and tidy) work are entirely appropriate. Privileges are often granted in the form of extra responsibility, e.g. taking messages to other teachers, looking after a new child, being the 'leader', and most teachers have stickers, stars and certificates of various kinds to award to children. In my experience, both of these incentives work extremely well. Children love to receive stickers and they positively shine with pride when they have successfully carried out a task for the teacher.

BUILDING SELF-ESTEEM

1. Being consistent in her approach to the children

Being consistent is one of the most important things to be when dealing with young children. Your child has come to rely on your reactions and knows that in certain situations, you will always respond in a similar way. Obviously there are links here with the setting of boundaries and what is acceptable to you, but being consistent isn't only connected with issuing disapproval, it is also about responding positively to your child when he has been helpful, kind, is trying hard and so on. He should also be able to feel confident in the belief that you will always give him the love he needs when he is feeling vulnerable, e.g. when he is fearful of a new situation or has hurt himself. Knowing that his parents will always do y in response to his doing x is very reassuring and gives him clear guidelines to work to. It is not always as easy to be consistent as it sounds but it is very important.

How can your teacher develop this approach?

She should be aware that it is also very important for her to keep her reactions and comments as consistent as she possibly can. As far as it is humanly possible, this means making sure she issues praise where praise is due, encouragement where encouragement is due, comfort where comfort is due and disapproval where disapproval is appropriate, in the same way and for similar things, each day. In this way, children come to know how to avoid 'bad' reactions and strive for 'good' ones.

2. Accepting children for the individuals they are

Your child is unique and is loved for who he is, regardless of what he can or can't do. Loving him in this non-judgemental way does not mean that you accept any unsociable behaviour that he displays, but it does mean that you love him as a special person, through successes and failures. It is very important to make this distinction between the person and the action. Children should not be made to feel that you do not love them any more because they have behaved in a certain way, however unacceptable that behaviour was.

How can your teacher develop this approach?

When he starts school, your child will need to be and will be treated as an individual. Your teacher will find out about his qualities, strengths, likes and dislikes, making it easier for her to respond to subtleties in his looks and behaviour as he settles into his new environment. She will have a class of very different pupils but they should all be made to feel equally important. She should endeavour to 'get through' to them all.

3. Being a friend and helping children to make new friendships

Your child will undoubtedly have made several friendships already. He will probably have had friends to his house and been to others' houses himself. He sees his parents as friends who are there to help and support him.

How can your teacher develop this approach?

She should very clearly and openly value friendships by being warm and friendly herself and by encouraging children to make friends and keep them. Children should take part in discussions about what makes a good friend and what we can all do to help each other if we are down. Following a spate of rather unkind behaviour in our class on one occasion, we wrote a class book about the kind of things which made people upset and what we could do about it. This is what we wrote:

'My friend was sad because:

- somebody said "I'm not going to be your friend any more"
- no one would play with her
- somebody pushed her over
- somebody said "you're too silly to ride a pony"
- somebody said "I've got something new you haven't"
- somebody said "I hate you".

What did I do?

- I took her to talk to the teacher.
- I listened carefully to her.
- I gave her a cuddle.
- I said "don't worry, I'll be your friend".
- I played with her and let her share my things.
- I drew a picture specially for her.
- I said sorry and decided to be nice to her every day.
- I said I'm very sorry. I won't do it ever again.'

Drawing attention to a problem in this way seemed very helpful. By discussing together and allowing all the children to imagine themselves in the role of the upset child, the class was encouraged to come up with these very suitable solutions.

4.   Treating the children with respect

Children should feel confident that they will be treated with respect. They are not babies any more but are rapidly developing into young adults with their own, very clear ideas. They are learning and absorbing far more at this time than at any other time in their lives. The rate of growth, both physically and mentally, is enormous. Therefore we should have nothing but tremendous respect for their ability to learn so much so quickly.

How can your teacher develop this approach?

She should not talk down to the children. This is illustrated strongly by the following little anecdote. We had a Victorian week at our school when the whole day was planned as it would have been in Victorian times. We decorated the room accordingly. All the children came to school in Victorian dress and were given Victorian names. The classes were named as they would have been at that time. I told the children that the Reception class used to be called 'Upper Babies'. A very affronted Reception class quickly protested – 'Oh rubbish!' So be warned, once children settle down at school, they have quite a high opinion of themselves and do not take kindly to being belittled.

5.   Giving the children lots of praise

Children respond well to praise and will most likely have been praised by you for trying hard, being kind, good behaviour, especially careful work and so on.

How can your teacher develop this approach?

Teachers have plenty of opportunity to issue praise and should use this technique as often as possible because it is a very positive teaching tool. Children love being praised as it draws attention to them and they are, at heart, quite self-centred at this young age. In contrast, they hate being ignored and this can also be a good teaching aid if bad behaviour needs to be discouraged.

Ideally, what will actually happen in the classroom?

The teacher will praise success, but not only academic success. She is likely to praise good behaviour, kindness to others, independence and responsibility as well as good work and should make a point of praising effort as well as the end result. For some children, the enormous degree of effort put into their work is not always reflected in the quality of the finished product. For others, who find it easy to produce neat work, an excellent result may be produced with very little effort. Praise needs to be issued accordingly.

6. Continuing to give them warmth and love

Your child has grown up feeling loved. He has received hugs and cuddles and has had his hand held in order to make him feel brave in new situations. Nothing is more natural than to want to touch and hug your young child and nothing is more reassuring for the child than receiving that warm love from you.

How can your teacher develop this approach?

Children should not, be deprived of this warmth when they are at school. Very sadly, the teaching world has become so fearful of legal action, that in some schools, it is now considered inappropriate for children to receive any physical contact at all. At the risk of being thought incorrect, I feel it is essential for children to continue to receive this kind of physical contact, certainly at this very young age. A child who is excited about something needs to have a hug. A child who has hurt himself needs a cuddle. A child who is wary of a new situation needs a reassuring hand. A child who is upset needs to have a quiet talk. I cannot see what harm there is in all that. Indeed, I can see a lot of harm in not doing it.

To deprive a child of any physical contact, when he is used to receiving it at home, is verging on the cruel, but is certainly very unfair. I think it is impossible to teach this young age group without showing children affection in this way and I would certainly feel I was letting them down if I did not do so. The undoubted cases of serious abuse must certainly be stamped out, but surely, they should not be allowed to influence and regulate what is, after all, a totally natural way to behave.

7. Continuing to respect their privacy

Children at home have their own space – be it their own room or one shared with a sibling. They know that they can keep their own possessions there and that they will be safe. It is their own private space. Children need their privacy and should be able to know that any secrets they choose to tell you will not be passed on to anyone else. Trust is built up in this way.

How can your teacher develop this approach?

Children should be able to trust their teachers. They will be able to do this if teachers are:

- open with their pupils and encourage them to share things with them
- non-judgemental and prepared to listen to all sides
- willing to give them time
- sensitive to their feelings
- aware of problems
- appreciative of the need for secrecy.

8. Helping them to see the world as it is

As your child grows up he needs to become more aware of the world as it is. At first, you will have protected him from knowing too much about the less desirable aspects of life, thus allowing his confidence to grow. However, we have a duty to protect children and, sadly, in this day and age, they soon have to know that there are 'bad' people out there, from whom they need protecting. It is not necessary to scare children unduly but they do need to know what they must and mustn't do when out and about.

How can your teacher develop this approach?

Schools and teachers will often ask the police to come and talk to young children about the 'Dangers of Strangers'. I have listened to quite a few of these discussions and, in my experience, they have always been extremely well done and greatly enjoyed by all the children. The police are seen as friends which is vital for children to know and the message is put across in a very simple fashion which makes it easy for the children to remember. I have also been very impressed by how much the children already know – obviously, you are also doing a good job!

This is not the only darker aspect of life and teachers also have to help them with illness, death, burglaries and all sorts of other things which unfortunately young children have to cope with all too soon. There are many ways of dealing with these, including allowing the child who has experienced the event to talk about it, and reading about similar experiences in books.

9. Allowing them enough freedom to make mistakes

We all make mistakes and most of us, hopefully, learn from these. Children need to know that it is acceptable to make mistakes. It is part of growing up. Adults also make mistakes and do things they regret, but they then try to put things right.

How can your teacher develop this approach?

Teachers are no different from anyone else. They make mistakes too and it is actually important that they do, as teachers need to be accessible to children. Someone who is always right about everything can appear to be a rather daunting figure. For a child, seeing a teacher making a mistake is valuable and reassuring so long as the teacher is seen to put this right and the issue does not become an occasion for giggling and lack of respect. If handled correctly, these can be positive learning experiences for children, helping them to avoid excessive guilt feelings when they have made mistakes.

7

Maintaining Good Relationships

It is in everyone's interests to maintain the good relationship you have been working so hard to create. The following points are important when considering how to maintain this good parent/teacher relationship. With constant effort and determination on both sides, this should be relatively easy to do.

GIVING MUTUAL SUPPORT AND ADMIRATION

Teachers are every bit as vulnerable as parents. They are also human beings! Therefore, it is important that both parents and teachers should give each other mutual support and admiration. As a teacher, it is always very encouraging to hear positive feedback from parents and to be given thanks for your hard work. The realisation that all your efforts have helped a child and are appreciated does an enormous amount to boost morale. As a parent, it is also very pleasing to be told when your child has done something especially good or helpful. It is difficult being a parent. You need to have your morale boosted as well!

HAVING TRULY POSITIVE EXCHANGES

Understand the real need for making some exchanges truly positive, without a hint of criticism anywhere – times for sharing happiness and success, whether home or school initiated. It is gratifying if your teacher tells you when she has had a particularly productive or happy day with your child and it is good to hear about his enthusiasm for a school trip, the growth of his recently planted seed or a favourite story. As a parent it is just as important that you should tell your teacher about some of your child's special activities and successes out of school. Let her share the excitement and issue congratulations as well.

RECOGNISING EMOTIONS

Recognise that you, as well as your children, have very real feelings. You are not immune to any of the common emotions of aggression, frustration, sadness, fear, jealousy, possessiveness and so on that you see in your children every day. You spend a great deal of time helping your children to deal with these feelings so why should you feel that you can just dismiss them in yourself? When parents and teachers meet up for discussions of whatever nature, these feelings need to be recognised and talked about, not just ignored.

ACKNOWLEDGING A FEAR OF CRITICISM

Many parents often feel nervous and inferior when they come into school. They can feel at a disadvantage because they are not on their home ground. Acknowledge these feelings as they well up all too easily. Uncertainty, worry and guilt are very common when meetings between parents and teachers are arranged to discuss potential problems. There seems to be an innate fear that such meetings between parents and teachers will inevitably involve some form of criticism or confrontation.

Why should this be so? After all, you have chosen your school, you have met the teacher, you liked what you saw . . . and yet! How do we overcome this? It needs to be firmly borne in mind that both teacher and parent are on the same side and working towards the same goals. This way, it will be much easier to work out a sensible strategy for solving the problem, if indeed there is one. Calm explanations from both sides should be given and sensitively listened to. Trying to imagine yourself in the other party's shoes can be a great help, as mentioned before, and is a useful policy to adopt. Remember that teachers can also be pretty nervous before parents' evenings and are equally wary of parental criticism!

TACKLING PROBLEMS EARLY

It is vital that potential problems are looked at early, before they develop into major issues. It is also very important that these potential problems are discussed *with* the teacher, *not* behind her back, with other parents. It is very easy for the facts of a situation to become horribly distorted when the school 'grapevine' gets going and rumours fly around the car park! It will not help you to put your concerns across convincingly if you arrive with a string of incorrect facts.

It can be tempting to leave what you perceive as a minor problem, hoping that it will go away. However, once even a minor problem has started to become an issue in your mind, it is unlikely to disappear unless it is tackled and talked about. Far better to air it quickly before the parties involved have got so upset by it that they can no longer deal with it rationally and sensibly. An early exploration of the issues will enable everyone to feel more in control and will hopefully solve the problem before it has time to take over.

QUESTIONS AND ANSWERS

I know my son can be very tricky. He is a handful and can be very rude. He is sometimes rough with other children. I am embarrassed and worried about hearing what he has done wrong. What should I do?

It is important to share your knowledge with the teacher. Acknowledge your embarrassment and your dread at hearing that he has been causing problems. You will find that the teacher will almost always be sympathetic as long as you give her the feeling that:

- you admit that there is a problem
- you also wish to sort out the problem
- you are not there to criticise.

She is not there to criticise either, but she will ask for your help and support when she tries to tackle these difficulties in whatever way she sees fit.

My daughter says she doesn't like school. I can't find out why. What should I do?

It is essential to share this information with your child's teacher as soon as possible. She is there to help. Many things can upset children who are new to school routine. The most common problems are:

- friendships – or lack of them
- playing in the playground
- teasing
- school dinners.

She will be able to tell you whether she feels your daughter is having difficulty with any of these. Unless your child is exceptionally good at hiding her feelings, most teachers will have sensed if there is a problem and will hopefully have told you about their concerns. Some children are in fact perfectly happy in school but manage to persuade their parents that they are miserable, much to the exasperation of both parents and teachers. On occasions, it is necessary to harden your heart and believe the school. It is also important to greet your child very positively at the end of the day, rather than giving her the opportunity to tell you how bad her day has been, by asking her worriedly if she has been all right. However, if you are still concerned and feel that there might be a bullying problem involving your child, you must obviously take it further.

My daughter doesn't want to read to me at home. This upsets me. What should I do?
Talk to your teacher and explain the problem. She may well suggest stopping asking your child to read at home altogether for a few days, allowing time for you both to calm down over the issue. Try not to let your child see that you are upset. Instead, read to *her*, letting her choose the books she wants you to read. This will maintain her interest in books. After a while it will probably be possible to reintroduce very short sessions of her reading, making sure you consider the following important points:

- Do not force the issue, turning it into a battleground, particularly when your child is obviously tired.

- Make sure you choose a time when you can give her your undivided attention – even five minutes of full attention is much better than fifteen minutes of half-hearted attention. Bear in mind that the very end of the day can be a time when you are both very tired and the morning can be very busy with everyone trying to get ready.

- Make sure your child has had a chance to unwind and relax at the end of the day. Give her something to eat and drink.

- Make sure that you are both sitting comfortably and, if at all possible, that other siblings are occupied elsewhere.

- Keep sessions short, stopping as soon as you sense your child has had enough.

Keep in touch with the teacher and let her know how things develop. She is there to support and help.

My son is always tired in the mornings. Is school too much for him? What should I do?
Again, speak to your teacher. See if she has noticed the same problem. If so, is he tired all the time, or just at the end of the day which is to be expected? Or is his tiredness a means of avoiding a particular aspect of school life he is not so keen on? Many children are brilliant at avoidance tactics. Is there more of a problem on any particular day when he has to undertake a particular activity? Depending on the answers to these questions, you can explore the matter further in order to sort out a problem or take a tougher attitude to his complaints. If there is no noticeable problem at school, it is also important to consider whether he is going to bed early enough. Is he getting enough sleep?

It is a real trial getting my daughter to school in the mornings. It is a battle to get her to wear the right clothes and she won't come into the classroom with me. I know she is playing me up. What should I do?
Enlist your teacher's help. It is often easier for her, not being directly involved or affected by the situation, to be firm. She also has the advantage of 'pulling rank' within the school setting. When children realise that they are not getting anywhere, they will usually quickly comply with what is required.

What do I do when my daughter clings to me and starts to scream when I try to leave her in the classroom?
Again, involve your teacher as soon as possible. This problem is not uncommon as children settle into their new school but can be very upsetting for parents. Teachers are very used to dealing with the problem and are able to keep relatively calm, despite having to deal with a loudly screaming child! Therefore, the best thing to do is to let the teacher cope, once you have said goodbye and reassured your child that you will be back later. This is, of course, a very difficult thing to do and I have every sympathy with parents who find it almost impossible. However, I can assure you that, as a teacher, even with the most determined child, I have never known a child scream for longer than five minutes. With a combination of gentle handling and diversionary tactics, they usually calm down remarkably quickly. In order to stop

this kind of behaviour as quickly as possible, it is important that you pick up your child at the end of the day in a positive frame of mind. If he sees you have been upset by his reaction, he is more likely to continue.

8

Vital Developments for the Future

DEVELOPING A SENSE OF HUMOUR AND AN ABILITY TO LAUGH

We find many things that children do amusing and they often make us laugh. I have seen some wonderful 'emergent' spellings during my years in the classroom:

- byootfl (beautiful)
- wobulie (wobbly)
- tercee (Turkey)
- brij (bridge)
- bkoz (because)
- chex (checks).

They still make me smile, but it must be remembered that for the child, this represents a tremendous leap forward in their understanding of phonetic spelling and is definitely not something to laugh at. Even though none of us mean it to be in any way degrading, it can seem that way to the child. So we need to be careful.

Great amusement was always caused in our school with the hymn 'Give me oil in my lamp. . . .', which has a chorus – 'Sing hosanna, Sing hosanna.' The children always sang with great gusto but with the words 'Sing Rosanna' (the name of one of the children in the class)!

Amusement can stem from finding something rather charming or it can sometimes stem from a sense of despair that things will never improve. Nativity plays are notorious for this. Rehearsals test the teacher's ability to keep a straight face as yet another, unexpected disaster arises, but these are definitely not the right occasions for laughter either!

Children can find accidents which happen to other people, such as the dropping of a pencil tin on the floor – especially the teacher's – a suitable occasion for peels of laughter. This also needs to be discouraged.

As adults, we are able to laugh at ourselves, but children should not be expected to be able to do this just yet. It is appropriate to laugh at some things we find amusing, but not all. When children think we are laughing at them but do not understand why, they can be very easily hurt. However, appropriate laughter *with* children, stemming from their understanding of a funny situation, e.g. in a book, an amusing story, when playing games and in discussions, can be very therapeutic and the development of a sense of humour is definitely something to encourage. Some children have an uninhibited, natural, sense of humour while others need to have this side of their characters developed. It will be developed and encouraged if children have plenty of opportunities to hear adults laughing and smiling amongst themselves, even if adult laughter can sometimes be rather more contrived.

Exercises

- Think up funny endings to Nursery Rhymes (e.g. Humpty Dumpty sat on a pin, then we heard a terrible din), or funny versions of well-known stories, using books such as Roald Dahl's *Revolting Rhymes* as stimulus. Enjoy laughing together as your rhymes and stories get more and more ridiculous.

- Draw strange looking characters and think up silly names for them.

DEVELOPING CONFIDENCE

Hopefully, having read this book and become more aware of what actually happens in schools, you will be feeling in a good position to help your child to feel confident about this new stage of his life. Children often reflect our feelings and if you are feeling more relaxed, your child should be too.

Children's confidence grows as they settle into their new school environment and begin to relax with the new people in it. School provides many opportunities for developing this confidence and teachers often find that they are inundated with volunteers for message carriers and children who want to take active parts in assemblies and so on, quite early on in the new term. The school environment makes such potentially daunting occasions as standing up in the hall and saying something much easier because they are never alone and there is always support from others in the class.

Most children of this age are not at all self-conscious when standing up in front of others. I remember a number of concerts and plays at our school when really young children stood up and sang solos in front of quite a big audience without batting an eyelid. It is only at a later stage, sadly, that this can become a problem.

Experiencing success

Nothing boosts confidence more readily for children than knowing that they have succeeded when trying to do something. It puts them in a good position to move on positively to the next challenge. Conversely, having failed once makes trying again and undertaking the next task more difficult. Therefore it is essential for both teachers and parents to make sure that their children experience plenty of success. This means plenty of challenges at the appropriate level for each child. Some will inevitably find certain aspects of the curriculum difficult. However, nearly all will find that they have a special ability somewhere else within the curriculum (e.g. art work, music, sport, design, etc.). If both teacher and parent can recognise and develop this ability, it will give the child confidence to tackle the areas he finds harder.

Building confidence in some children is not so easy. It can take a long time and require enormous patience.

CASE STUDY

James was a bright child and certainly had no problems understanding. He was, however, very shy, very quiet and reluctant to make eye contact when he first came to school. Although taking pride in his work, he found it very difficult to accept praise and quickly became uncomfortable if too much attention was given to him. What was the best way to increase James' confidence so that he felt more comfortable in his new environment?

To my mind, the answer lay in a softly, softly, slowly, slowly approach and an approach that provided James with plenty of exciting activities during the school day so that he was able to forget his discomfort. For the first few weeks, James sat with the rest of the group and appeared to pay attention. He listened carefully to all explanations and produced careful, neat work. However, he was clearly still tense, immediately looking away when I made any form of eye contact. Gradually, after a number of weeks, things began to change. James relaxed and began to talk more freely with his friends, although still rather wary of older children and adults. He enjoyed the various activities we provided for him and was obviously keen to know more. It was interesting to see how he would resolve the conflict between his desire for knowledge and his lack of confidence.

Eventually, after a couple of months, his desire for knowledge won over and he began to ask and answer questions 'through' his friends. He also began to produce his own work to put up in the classroom and seemed pleased when I was pleased. It was clear that James was gaining in confidence all the time. The next term, he was a rather different boy – much more confident and very highly motivated.

Exercises

● Maintain your child's interest when playing competitive games by keeping the level of play fairly even at first. He must be allowed to win some of the time if he is to build up his confidence sufficiently to keep going. He needs to believe that there is a possibility of him winning, but also that it is not disastrous for him to lose. Watching your positive reaction to losing will help him to understand this. Try to involve him in non-competitive activities as well – those which involve co-operation, such as puzzles or building a model – where the emphasis is on enjoyment, not on one or other person winning.

● It is important for children to spend time on whatever they enjoy doing. In reality, these days, this will probably be watching TV, playing computer games or playing with the latest craze, much though you may wish it was otherwise. It is up to you to regulate how much time you are prepared for your child to spend on these activities, but it is also important that you appear to be interested and involved in these, even if they leave you rather cold! In an ideal world, you would probably sit down and watch with them, but just to know who some of the characters are and what they get up to indicates your interest. This is very important for building confidence. If he feels you are involved in these activities, he may be more willing to take part in things you feel he should be doing, be it outside sporting activities, music, drama, art, swimming etc. With these, it is equally important to be interested and involved and to praise the results of his efforts. You may, of course, be lucky and have children who are untouched by TV or the latest craze, in which case, make the most of it!

DEVELOPING TOLERANCE

Children need to understand that others' looks, views and ways of doing things may well be different from theirs. We need to encourage young children to look beyond outward appearances and accept differences so that they can value the real person underneath. This is a vital lesson and needs to be established early. By doing this, they will come to realise that the world is a richer place because of all the different people in it, who all contribute in their own ways. Just as they are important, so is everyone else in this world.

Exercises

- Encourage an interest in and understanding of other people, other countries, other cultures, other festivals and celebrations by talking about holiday destinations, reading books together, watching television programmes and by talking to others who can tell you about them.

- Remember that your child will learn tolerance from you.

DEVELOPING RELIABILITY

It may seem strange to be talking about reliability in such young children, but by encouraging children to undertake jobs in the classroom, which many teachers do, you can begin to develop this. Children who are trusted with carrying out certain tasks will take great pride in doing them and will certainly remind the teacher if she forgets to give them enough time to do so. In a busy classroom, there is an enormous amount to remember in the course of a full day and watering the plants or, giving out invitations can easily get forgotten. However, you can usually rely on several children to remind you of what was supposed to happen. Children have a great ability to remember what is important to them. If you start from this point, where children have a vested interest in being reliable (remembering to tell the teacher), it is possible to gradually develop reliability into other areas which are perhaps more important to others, for instance remembering everything for school or tidying their bedrooms. Helping children to become people whom others can rely on is a very valuable thing to do.

Exercise

● Give your child specific, achievable and realistic jobs to do at home – ones which need doing regularly and ones which make a difference to people or pets if they are not done. Provide supervision if necessary. For example, make him responsible for feeding his pet at least twice a day. He will then come to realise that if he doesn't do this, the pet will become very unhappy as he is relying on your child to feed him regularly.

DEVELOPING PATIENCE

Children are not known for their patience. Most want instant gratification and can be quite demanding. However, once they start school, they will quickly realise they cannot always have what they want straight away. It is simply not possible for the teacher to attend to everyone at the same time. At first, this will no doubt be very frustrating to them, but soon it will help them to learn that they can still have the same outcome, even if they have to wait a little for it. This is a very valuable lesson for them to learn and one which will be increasingly useful in the future.

Exercises

● Do not 'drop everything' in order to respond to your child's demands. Make him wait if you are busy with something else when he wants attention.

● When your child has friends round to his house for tea, encourage him to offer cakes and biscuits to everyone else first, before he has one himself.

● When you have promised to buy something for your child and you have gone to the shops, complete your shopping first and make your child wait before going to the toy shop.

● Let your child see you being patient as you listen carefully to what he is saying and try to answer his questions.

DEVELOPING EMPATHY

Being able to show empathy – in other words, being able to understand and 'put oneself in another's shoes' – is a very useful attribute and helps children and adults to make real, lasting friendships. Young children are naturally quite self-centred and find it difficult to imagine what others are feeling, so we need to help them.

Exercises

- Point out what younger brothers or sisters might be feeling when they are not allowed to play with his toys. How could he help them?

- Explain how his friend who has no one to play with in the playground might be feeling. What could he do?

- Discuss the various characters in books you have read or programmes you have watched together. What were they feeling at various points in the story?

9

Personal Reflections

BEING A TEACHER OF YOUNG CHILDREN

It is wonderful to see children's excitement and natural enthusiasm for new things. When a child finally manages to do something he has up to now found very difficult, nothing can be more satisfying than to feel that you have played some part in this. Children of this age, at the beginning of their school careers, are rather like blotting paper, soaking up everything they are given. They are hungry for information and absorb an enormous amount in a very short time. The responsibilities to meet that need and to feed that appetite are quite considerable and certainly require every ounce of your energy and ingenuity. On the whole, children of this age are keen to learn which makes life easier, but there is certainly no let up in the intensity of the job as a result because there are also constant demands. You cannot set a group of these children a task and sit back while they get on with it by themselves. There is always someone who needs further explanation, encouragement, chivvying or attention because he has lost his book or broken his pencil!

BEING A PARENT OF YOUNG CHILDREN

I suppose my memories have faded somewhat after 20-plus years, but I can still remember many 'highs' and 'lows'. Amongst the 'lows' were the never-ending demands, the squabbles, the everlasting testing of the boundaries, trying to answer the endless 'why?' with anything other than 'because I say so!', the battles over food, the mess – and our Brahms' lullaby musical box which we had to play every night in order to get our eldest daughter to go to sleep! I fear it will never be the same for me again – or her, sadly! The single thing I found most difficult was the whining. I suppose I still do!

'Highs' included lots of laughter and giggling, the love and warmth, the natural excitement and enthusiasm of young children, the trips to museums, parks and the seaside, the imaginary games we had to join in, the magic shows or plays put on for our enjoyment at Christmas, wonderful home-made presents, and the satisfaction of seeing our children grow up and gradually become more independent. Parenthood is all about retreating slowly and gracefully and allowing children to take on more and more responsibility for themselves.

In other words – rewarding, satisfying, daunting, exhausting...! Parents and teachers have a great deal in common after all!

I was once asked by a child in my class how many children I had. 'Three,' I replied. 'Gosh,' said the little girl. 'Do you manage to cope?' Well . . . yes, actually! Even my memories of being a parent of three young children didn't manage to put me off taking on rather more than that as a teacher. There is nothing like it!

Appendix 1
Advice on Packed Lunches

Children need a great deal of energy to get through the school day and it is obviously advantageous to them if they eat a healthy, balanced meal at lunchtime. If your child has opted out of having school dinner, in favour of packed lunches, it is important to consider the contents of his lunchbox. His meal should include:

- carbohydrate – bread, pasta, rice or crackers
- protein and dairy products – cheese, milk, yoghurt, meat, chicken, fish or egg
- fruit or vegetables
- only a small amount of sugary food
- a drink.

To prepare him for eating with others at school:

- Try to make sure that your child is used to eating savoury food first and ending his meal with fruit or sweeter things.
- Always provide him with a drink at mealtimes and encourage him to finish it.

From your child's point of view, he will feel much more comfortable eating his lunch if he likes what he has been given and is able to manage it for himself. From the teacher's point of view, it makes for a much happier lunchtime if the following points are noted:

- Provide your child with a lunchbox which he can open and close easily.
- Name his lunch box clearly, make sure he can read this and use some other identifying mark as well, to make sure he finds his own lunch and not someone else's.

- Make sure that all drinks are either in plastic bottles, plastic screw-top containers or cartons. Show your child how to open and close bottles and containers and show him how to pierce cartons with a straw. Close containers firmly, but not so tightly that he cannot open them.

- If necessary, provide plastic spoons for yoghurts etc.

You might find the following tips helpful (from my experience of watching children eating their packed lunches in school):

- Use kitchen foil for wrapping sandwiches, rather than cling film – it is much easier to remove.

- Provide yoghurt in pots rather than in foil tubes, which tend to squirt everywhere!

- Make sure cartons of drink are accompanied by straws.

- Please do not expect teachers to peel apples. Encourage your child to eat them as they come or provide them ready peeled.

- Do not make school lunch the occasion for giving your child something you know he is reluctant to eat or has not eaten before .

- Do not give your child too much to eat. Children have a relatively short time in which to eat their lunch and they can be put off the whole idea if they have too much to get through.

Further information from *The Lunchbox Book*, Jenny Elkan (Southgate Publishers).

Appendix 2
Literacy and Numeracy Hours

Virtually all Primary schools now incorporate Literacy and Numeracy Hours into their daily curriculum. In Independent schools, the degree to which the formal structure is adhered to depends on the individual school.

The Literacy Hour consists of the following parts:

1. A session with the teacher teaching the children as a whole class.

2. A session with the children working in groups or individually –independent work or assisted by the teacher.

3. A short feedback session to reinforce the points that have been learned.

Examples of whole class work:

● Guided reading, using a variety of Big Books (fiction, non-fiction and poetry), looking carefully at individual words.

● Speaking in front of and listening to the whole class.

● Identifying rhyming words.

● Looking at the sound individual letters and groups of letters make.

● Learning easy spellings.

● Learning basic vocabulary to be recognised by sight.

● Practising the formation of letters.

● Learning new vocabulary.

Examples of smaller group and individual work:

● Practising holding a pencil correctly.

● Practising the formation of letters and doing simple writing exercises, including writing their own names.

● Recognising words and beginning to read using simple phonic reading rules.

The Numeracy Hour is less formally structured, but is usually split into three parts:

1. A short session of oral and mental maths with the whole class.

Children hear and are encouraged to use a wide variety of different mathematical vocabulary, for example, add/sum of/altogether/total etc. They practise counting forwards and backwards and working out simple problems in their heads.

2. A main session with the children working together as a whole class and also in small groups or individually, at appropriate levels.

In this session, the children learn new concepts and also practise work already covered.

3. A short session reinforcing all that has been learned.

To find out more, visit the following web sites:

www.parents.dfee.gov.uk

www.standards.dfee.gov.uk/literacy/teaching_resources

Appendix 3
Sample Report

Schools will obviously have different formats for their reports, but they will all give you an overview of how your child is progressing in the various parts of the curriculum at school.

REPORT FOR SAM SMITH – AUTUMN TERM 200X

Language Work

During whole class discussions, Sam always listens carefully. He is keen to answer questions and talk about his experiences.

He can recognise the sounds of individual letters and is beginning to make these sounds into words. He has started reading and is very keen. *Encouragement to read and look at books at home will help to reinforce his progress.*

At the moment, he is holding his pencil rather awkwardly and *it would be very helpful if he could be encouraged to hold it firmly between his thumb and first two fingers.* He is forming a number of letters incorrectly and *extra practice forming letters in groups of similar formation e.g. o,a,c,d,g,q and r,n,m,h would be very beneficial.*

Number Work

During whole class work, Sam takes an active part and is able to answer correctly. However, when working on his own, he lacks concentration and is easily distracted, causing him to make rather too many mistakes. *He would benefit from extra practice counting accurately, using counters, buttons or coins, touching each object as he counts it. It would also be very helpful if he could be encouraged to think in terms of which group has more and which has less.*

Social Development

Sam has settled in very well. He is very enthusiastic and has plenty of friends but *he can sometimes be a little rough in the playground.* He is always keen to help in the classroom.

Creative Learning

Sam loves painting and craft sessions and produces some very interesting work.

Physical Development

Sam enters into all games and P.E. with great enthusiasm and energy. He has good control of his body.

Attitude to Learning

Sam is keen to learn. He has undoubted energy and enthusiasm *but he needs to develop his concentration skills in order to produce his best work.* He generally has a very positive attitude towards school work.

In the above sample report, I have highlighted the points in italic where the teacher is asking for your help in reinforcing what she is trying to do. If there are areas where you do not understand what is being said, you should ask the teacher for clarification.

Appendix 4
Home/School Contracts

The main purpose of this book is to build trust between home and school. It will hopefully:

- encourage you to feel firmly committed to your school

- leave you with a will to do all you can to help with the education of your child

- leave you with a belief that the teacher and the school are working in the best interests of your child.

Many schools are now formalising these commitments by asking parents and schools to sign a Home/School agreement. These vary in complexity, but will ask for your support for the basic ethos and values of the school. More specifically, it may set out targets for both the school and for parents.

The School will:

- teach to a good standard, stimulating and challenging children of different abilities

- measure progress and feed-back the results to parents

- give appropriate levels of homework

- encourage good behaviour and discourage bad

- establish good contact between home and school.

As a Parent I will:

- make sure my child arrives in good time and attends regularly

- support the school's expectations with regard to behaviour and standards of work

- keep in touch with the school about any concerns I may have about my child

- read progress reports, attend parents' evenings and act on them.

Glossary

These examples of terminology and jargon are included so that you can warn your children what to expect and so that you can understand what the teachers are saying to you. Apologies for any unnecessary explanations!

COMMONLY USED WORDS IN THE CLASSROOM

Aprons/overalls
Assembly
Blackboard/whiteboard, board rubber
Cloakroom
Exercise books – books for written work
Flash cards – pieces of card with words written on for the children to recognise by sight
Folders – for reading books
Line up – single file/in pairs
Monitors – book, door etc. – children chosen to tidy up the book corner, hold the door open, etc.
PE – Physical Education (PE plimsolls/shoes, PE bags)
Position words – on, in, beside, by, next to, between, above, below
Register
Silence!!
Stapler/staples, drawing pins, masking tape, paper clips
Words for loo – loos/toilets/cloakroom

JARGON

Early Learning Goals – just as the government have set a National Curriculum for older children, they have outlined a number of Early Learning Goals for younger children between the ages of three and six, at the Foundation Stage. These set out the goals that children should reach by the time they are six and starting Year 1. These Early Learning Goals include skills in:

Creative Development Art and Music.

Knowledge and Understanding of the World History, Geography, Technology and Science.

Communication, Language and Literacy Reading, writing, speaking and listening.

Mathematical Development All number-related work

Personal, Social and Emotional Development Learning how to socialise, to share and to value and respect others.

Physical Development PE and Games.

Assessment How well your child is doing.

Audio-visual skills Ability to listen while looking at something and make the connection between the two.

Communication skills Learning how to speak and listen.

Comparative language Smaller, bigger, etc.

Fine Motor Development Holding such things as pencils correctly.

Formation of letters and numbers The correct way of writing these.

Gross Motor Development Body movements such as running, jumping, skipping, etc.

Hand/eye co-ordination Learning to follow patterns with a pencil or cut along lines with scissors.

Interacting socially Playing nicely, sharing and talking together.

Mathematical language Not only add/subtract etc. but also spend, altogether, hide, total, etc.

Onset and rhyme The two parts of a word, separated into its initial sound (the onset) and its rhyming part (the rhyme), e.g. s-at, c-at, p-at.

Overall development Growing up to be a rounded human being.

Personal, social and emotional needs What children need to keep them happy.

Phonetic approach Looking at the sounds letters make as opposed to their real names.

Position language Beside, on, in, etc.

Sequencing Sorting things into a logical order.

Short-term memory Ability to recognise patterns or words seen a few moments ago.

Sight words Words which need to be recognised by sight as they cannot be worked out phonetically e.g. the, here, was, etc.

To reach his full potential To do his best.

Topics A way of combining subjects, such as History, Geography, Science and other subjects, under one heading to make the learning process more meaningful to young children.

Using the senses To listen, look, touch and if appropriate, smell and taste, all at the same time, in order to reinforce learning.

Further Reading

Good Pre-School Activity Books.
Designed for parents to use at home with their children, these books all contain a variety of activities for practising early language and number work

Hodder Home Learning Workbooks – helping you prepare your child for school (Hodder and Stoughton)
Hodder Home Learning – Phonic Story Books – for beginner readers (Hodder and Stoughton) (supported by the National Confederation of Parent Teacher Associations -NCPTA)

Activities to help your child (Letts)
Numeracy Basics – Pre-school (Letts)

Let's Learn at home (Scholastic)
Skills for Early Years (Scholastic)

Parents' Essentials – for your 3–5 year old child (How To Books)

New Oxford Workbooks – Pre-School Practice (Oxford University Press).

Pre-School Workbooks – several new series available soon (Schofield and Sims)

Three schemes teaching the sounds of letters – phonics:

There are many ways of teaching phonics so it is worth checking with your school for their recommendations.

Letterland (Collins)

Jolly Phonics – The Phonics Handbook, Sue Lloyd (Jolly Learning Ltd.)

Super Phonics, Ruth Miskin (Hodder and Stoughton)

Early Schooling

Starting School, Dr Richard Woolfson (Thorsons).

A Parents' Guide to Key Stage 1, Shirley Clarke and Barry Silsby (Hodder Home Learning).

Starting School Parent Guide, Geraldine Taylor (Ladybird).

Longman Parents' Guides - Key Stage 1, Ted Wragg (Longman).

Helping Your Child Succeed in School, Michael Popkin, Bettie B. Youngs, Jane M. Healy (Active Parenting Publishers).

Helping Your Child to Learn at Primary School, Polly Bird (How To Books)

Pre-school Planner, (The Stationery Office).

The Lunchbox Book, Jenny Elkan (Southgate Publishers).

Learning Difficulties

Asperger's Syndrome – a guide for parents and professionals, Tony Attwood (Jessica Kingsley Publishers).

Autism and Asperger Syndrome, edited by Ura Frith, (Cambridge University Press).

How to Detect and Manage Dyslexia, Philomena Ott (Heinemann).

Day to Day Dyslexia in the Classroom, Joy Pollock and Elisabeth Waller (Routledgefalmer).

Overcoming Dyslexia, Dr Beve Hornsby (Vermilion).

Dyslexia and Other Learning Difficulties – The Facts, Mark Selikowitz (OUP).

Developmental Dyspraxia, Madeleine Portwood (David Fulton).

'Your Child' series (Element):

   Dyslexia, Robin Temple (Element).

   Hyperactivity - What's the Alternative?, Maggie Jones (Element).

Hyperactive Child, Belinda Barnes and Irene Colquhoun (Thorsons).

Understanding ADHD, Dr Christopher Green and Dr Kit Chee (Vermilion).

An Introduction to Children with Special Educational Needs, Michael Alcott (Hodder and Stoughton).

Bullying

The Anti-Bullying Handbook, Keith Sullivan (OUP).

The Parents Book about Bullying – changing the course of your child's life, William Voors (Hazelden).

Bullying, Jenny Alexander (Element).

Coping with Bullying, (CD Rom, Rotary International).

101 Ways to Deal With Bullying, Michaele Elliott (Hodder and Stoughton).

How to Help Your Child Overcome Bullying, Sheila Munro (Piccadilly Press).

Helping Children Cope With Bullying, Sarah Lawson (Sheldon Press).

Helping Hands - Pay Up Or Else, Anne de Bode, Rien Broere (Evans Brothers).

MYBees: Stop Picking On Me, Pat Thomas (Hodder Wayland).

No More Bullying, Rosemary Stones (HappyCat Books).

Wise Guides Bullying, Michele Elliott (Hodder and Stoughton).

Twins

Starting School - Together or Apart? The Twins and Multiple Birth Association (TAMBA).

Parenting

The Parentalk Guide to the Childhood Years, Steve Chalke, (Hodder and Stoughton).

Parentalk's How To Succeed as a Parent, Steve Chalke (Hodder and Stoughton).

Love, Laughter and Parenting, Steve and Shaaron Biddulph (Dorling Kindersley).

The Secret of Happy Children, Steve Biddulph (Thorsons).

More Secrets of Happy Children, Steve Biddulph with Shaaron Biddulph (Thorsons).

Positive Parenting, Elizabeth Hartley-Brewer (Vermilion).

Confident Children, Gael Lindenfield (Thorsons).

How To Raise a Happy Child, Javad H. Kashani (Vermilion).

Raising Happy Children, Jan Parker and Jan Stimpson (Hodder and Stoughton).

Saying 'No', Asha Phillips (Faber and Faber).

Raising the Successful Child, Sylvia Clare (How To Books).

Paranoid Parenting, Frank Furedi (Penguin).

The Good Child Guide, Dr Noel Swanson (Aurum).

Self-esteem for Boys/Self-esteem for Girls – or raising happy and confident children, Elizabeth Hartley-Brewer (Vermilion).

How to behave so your children will too, Dr Sal Severe (Vermilion).

Parenting Pre-School Children, Paul Stallard (How To Books).

The Secrets of Successful Parenting, Andrea Clifford-Poston (How To Books).

Physical Disabilities
Allergies, Brigid McConville and Dr Rajendra Sharma (Element).
Asthma, Erika Harvey (Element).
Eczema, Maggie Jones (Element).
Diabetes, Catherine Steven (Element).

Useful Addresses and Web Sites

GENERAL

Education

The Department for Education and Employment, Sanctuary Buildings, Great Smith Street, Westminster, London, SW1P 3BT Tel: 0870 0012345
www.parents.dfee.gov.uk
www.bbc.co.uk/education

Qualifications and Curriculum Authority (QCA), 29 Bolton Street, London W1Y 7PD
www.qca.org.

Advisory Centres for Education (ACE), 1C Aberdeen Studios, 22–24 Highbury Grove, London N5 2DQ
www.ace-ed.co.uk

Parenting

Parentline 0808 800 2222
www.parentlineplus.org.uk
www.practicalparent.org.uk
www.bbc.co.uk/education/health/chs (health and food)
www.familiesandwork.org
www.nfpi.org

Dealing with bullying

Childline 0800 111 111
www.childline.org.

Kidscape, 152 Buckingham Palace Road, London, SW1 9TR
Tel: (0202) 7730 3300
www.kidscape.org.uk

The Anti-Bullying Campaign, 10 Borough High Street, SE1 90Q
Tel: (020) 7378 1446
www.bbc.co.uk/education/bully/index.htm
www.nspcc.org.uk

SPECIAL EDUCATIONAL NEEDS

Centre for Studies on Integration in Education (CSIE), 1 Redland
Close, Elm Lane, Redland, Bristol BS6 6UE
Tel: (0117) 923 8450
(advice about including children with special needs in mainstream
schools)
www.parents.dfee.gov.uk /sen/parin.htm (Special Educational Needs)

Gifted Children
National Association for Gifted Children, 540 Elder House, Milton
Keynes MK9 1LR
Tel: (01908) 673677
www.rmplc.co.uk/orgs/nagc

MENSA Foundation for Gifted Children, Mensa House, St. John's
Square, Wolverhampton, WV2 4AH
www.mensa.org.uk/mfgc

Dyspraxia
The Dyspraxia Foundation, 8 West Alley, Hitchin, Herts, SG5 1EG
Tel: (01462) 454986
www.emmbrook.demon.co.uk/dysprax/homepage.htm

Dyslexia
Dyslexia Institute, 133 Gresham Road, Staines, Middlesex TW18 2AJ
Tel: (01784) 463851
www.dyslexia-inst.org.uk
British Dyslexia Association, 98 London Road, Reading, Berkshire,
RG1 5AU
Tel: (01189) 668271
Helen Arkell Dyslexia Centre, Frensham, Farnham, Surrey GU10 3BW
Tel: (01252) 792400

Attention Deficit Hyperactivity Disorder (ADHD) and Attention Deficit Disorder (ADD)

The Overload Network International, Flat 1, 58 North Fort Street, Edinburgh, E87 HMP
Tel: (0131) 555 4967
www.overloadnetwork.org.uk

Speech and Language Impairment

AFASIC – Unlocking Speech and Language, 69–85 Old Street, London EC1V 9HX
www.afasic.org.uk
ICAN, The national educational charity for children with speech and language difficulties, 4 Dyer's Buildings, Holborn, London EC1N 2QP
Tel: (0870) 010 4066
Royal College of Speech and Language Therapists, 2 White Hart Yard, London SE1 1NX
Tel: (020) 7378 1200

Hearing Impairment

The National Deaf Children's Society, 15 Dufferin Street, London EC1Y 8UR
Tel: (020) 7250 0123
www.ndcs.org.uk

Visual Impairment

The Royal National Institute for the Blind (RNIB), 224 Great Portland Street, London W1N 6AA
Tel: (020) 7388 1266

Autism

The National Autistic Society, 393 City Road, London, EC1V 1NE
Tel: (020) 7833 2299
www.oneworld.org/autism-uk

Down's Syndrome

The Down Syndrome Educational Trust, The Sarah Duffen Centre, Belmont Street, Southsea, Portsmouth, Hampshire PO5 1NA
Tel: (023) 9282 4261
www.downsnet.org
Down's Syndrome Association, 155 Mitcham Road, London, SW17 9PG
Tel: (020) 8682 4001

Emotional and Behavioural Difficulties
The Association of Workers for Children with Emotional and Behavioural Difficulties, Charlton Court, East Sutton, Maidstone, Kent ME17 3DQ
Tel: (01622) 843 104

Cystic Fybrosis
Cystic Fibrosis Trust, 11 London Road, Bromley, Kent BR1 1BY
Tel: (020) 8464 7211

Epilepsy
British Epilepsy Association, Anstey House, 40 Hanover Square, Leeds LS3 1BE
Tel: 0800 309030

Cerebral Palsy
SCOPE, 6–10 Market Road, London, N7 9PW
Tel: (020) 7619 7100
www.scope.org.uk

Royal Society for Mentally Handicapped Children and Adults (MENCAP) Mencap National Centre, 123 Golden Lane, London EC1Y 0RT
Tel: (020) 7454 0454

Council for Disabled Children, 8 Wakeley Street, London, EC1V 7QE
Tel: (020) 7843 6000

The British Psychological Society
Tel: (0116) 254 9568
www.bps.org.uk

Child Consultants
Tel: (020) 7637 3177
www.childconsultants.com

John Acklaw, Educational Psychology Service
Tel: (01621) 743020
www.eps.anglianet.co.uk

Association of Educational Psychologists, 26 The Avenue, Durham, DH1 4ED

Index

aggression, 34, 35
apologising, 58
Attention Deficit Disorder, 29
availability, 68

Baseline Assessment, 44
being aware, 56
boundaries, 60
bullying, 29, 31, 85

case studies, 35, 55, 57, 90
challenges, 72, 73
choosing schools,
   what to ask, 16
   what to look for, 15
collection time, 24, 25, 41
common sense, 60
communication, 56
complaints,
   children's, 31, 32, 36, 37
   parents, 37, 38
concentration, 54, 55
confidence, 11, 89, 90–92
consistency, 46, 76
coping strategies, 30–35
curiosity, 52

Early Learning Goals, 26
empathy, 94
encouragement, 67
enthusiasm, 53
exercises, 89, 91–94
expectations,
   of children, 42–44
   of parents, 39–42
   of teachers, 44–47
explanations, 49, 50, 66, 67

fear, 33, 34
   of criticism, 83
feelings, 24, 83
   difficult, 32, 33
first few days, 24, 25, 26
first impressions, 14
Foundation Stage, 26
freedom, 68, 81
friendships, 55, 77, 78
frustration, 34, 35
fun, 69, 71

getting information, 46
giving information, 39
good and bad behaviour, 59, 84
good manners, 61, 62

happiness, 69, 70
home/school contracts, 103, 104
homework, 40, 46
honesty, 61

illness, 42
imagination, 74, 75
incentives, 75
independence, 54
individuality, 76
involvement, 41

jealousy, 34, 36

Literacy Hour, 99, 100
loneliness, 34

mistakes, 81
motivation, 52, 73
moving schools, 18

mutual
  understanding, 9
  support, 82
  admiration, 82

National Curriculum, 26, 27
Numeracy Hour, 100

over-subscribed schools, 18

packed lunches, 97, 98
parent/teacher discussions, 44, 45
parting from your child, 20, 22, 86
patience, 93
Personal and Social Development, 10
playground, 37
possiveness, 34, 36
praise, 78, 79
pressure, 66
privacy, 79
problems,
  children's, 29, 30
  parent/teacher, 21, 83, 84

questions and answers, 84–87

relationships,
  children's, 32
  parent/teacher, 10, 21, 23, 24, 82

reliability, 92
reports, 40, 101, 102
respect, 78
responsibility, 63
right and wrong, 61
roles,
    parental, 22, 23, 48
    teacher, 23

safety, 68
school meals, 36
self-esteem, 29, 30, 76
sense of humour, 88
settling-in
  what to expect, 20
sharing, 36, 58, 59
shyness, 55, 90
spontaneity, 70
stranger danger, 80
stress, 9, 21

teasing, 29, 32, 72
tolerance, 92
trust, 10, 23, 39, 80

uniform, 37, 86

working partnership, 10, 39